ADVENTURES
WITH
A HAND LENS

ADVENTURES
WITH
A HAND LENS

RICHARD HEADSTROM

Illustrated by the Author

Dover Publications, Inc., New York

Published in Canada by General Publishing Company, Ltd., 30 Lesmill Road, Don Mills, Toronto,
Ontario.
Published in the United Kingdom by Constable
and Company, Ltd., 10 Orange Street, London WC 2.

This Dover edition, first published in 1976, is an
unabridged and slightly revised republication of the
work originally published by J. B. Lippincott Company, New York, in 1962.

International Standard Book Number: 0-486-23330-8
Library of Congress Catalog Card Number: 76-10910

Manufactured in the United States of America
Dover Publications, Inc.
180 Varick Street
New York, N. Y. 10014

TO MY WIFE

In Appreciation of Her Help and Devotion

CONTENTS

7

UNTIL ONLY A FEW YEARS AGO, as time is measured, man had lived on the earth unaware of what existed in the heavens, unaware of how plants and animals are put together, unaware of the countless numbers of tiny plants and animals that exist everywhere but are invisible to the naked eye. He could see and study only what was apparent. When his eyesight faded he was doomed to grope about in a world he could but dimly perceive.

Then, somewhere, someone happened to look through a piece of curved glass. Today we need not grope our way when eyesight begins to fade, nor suffer the results of defective vision. We can peer into the far reaches of the heavens and look at faraway stars and planets, we can study microscopic plants and animals, we can examine the cells of our bodies, we can record for our children and our grandchildren happenings in our own lives, and for posterity world-wide events as they occur, we can sit in our homes and be transported to places miles away and watch a sports spectacle or a political convention or some other event in progress. By means of a piece of curved glass, which came to be called a lens because it is shaped like a lentil, we can look at countless things we never suspected existed, or, if we do know of their existence, what they actually look like, for many of these things appear quite different, when viewed through such a piece of glass, from the way they appear to the naked eye.

And what do we call such a piece of glass? We call it a magnifying glass. But it has other names, too, such as hand lens, pocket magnifier, or reading glass. Whatever it is called, we can buy one almost anywhere for a few pennies to a few dollars, depending on its magnifying power.

Folding pocket magnifiers made by Bausch and Lomb may be purchased with one, two, or three lenses and are perfect for viewing a wide variety of natural objects. Thus you may get a pocket magnifier with one lens having a magnification of three or five times; a magnifier with a double lens having a magnification of either three to seven times, four to nine times, or five to twelve times;

or a magnifier with a triple lens having a magnification of five to twenty times.

Somewhat more expensive models are the Coddington magnifier and the Hastings magnifier. Both may be obtained with magnifications of seven, ten, fourteen, and twenty times. A reading glass, also made by Bausch and Lomb, has a magnification of three times, and comes in different sizes with different focuses: one with a diameter of two and a half inches has a six-inch focus; one with a diameter of three and a quarter inches has a focus of eight inches; one with a diameter of four inches has a focus of ten inches; and one with a diameter of five inches has a thirteen-inch focus. The focus indicates the distance the lens must be held from an object to get a clear image.

So let us get a magnifier or hand lens and turn to the first Adventure and then to the others that follow. We shall discover many interesting things and have fun doing so.

*We Peer through
Our Lens at Some
Familiar Objects*

For our first adventure we shall examine a few things we can find around the house. And what can we better start with than the paper on which these words are printed? Examine it with your hand lens or pocket magnifier. Next examine a piece of newspaper and then a piece of glossy paper from one of the better magazines, and finally compare all three with a piece of blotting paper. In which paper do you find a network of loose fibers? I think you will agree that in the blotting paper the fibers are more in evidence and that there are larger spaces between them. This is the secret of the blotting paper's action in absorbing ink. It all has to do with capillarity, which we can define simply as the creeping of a liquid into a very narrow space, and that is just about what the ink does when it passes into the blotting paper.

Now look at a piece of fabric and see how it appears under a lens. Hold up to the light a towel, or shirt, or skirt, or handkerchief and examine a section of it with your lens. You will observe threads running crosswise. (*Figure 1*). The threads running lengthwise are called the warp; those running crosswise the woof. It is said that the number of threads per inch is an indication of quality or strength. Select a square-inch area of any fabric and count the number of threads in the woof. A high thread count indicates good quality or that the fabric is strong and will wear well; a low thread count indicates the opposite. While you are still holding the fabric to the light, note if there is any unevenness in the weave. If there are spots which appear thinner than others or if the fabric is woven unevenly, the material will wear unevenly.

Most of us regard an egg merely as an article of food, and though we all know that a chicken can be hatched from it we give little thought to this miracle. You will learn how an egg is put together and how a plant or animal develops from it. For the present all

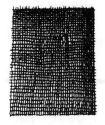

Figure 1
SECTION OF FABRIC

Figure 2
GROUND COFFEE

Figure 3
INSTANT COFFEE

we are interested in is the shell of our breakfast egg.

A chicken can be hatched from it, but only under certain conditions. First of all the egg has to be a fertile one, and secondly it has to be incubated. That the developing chick may have air, there must be some way for the air to enter the egg. There must also be some way for waste gases to escape, for every living thing gives off waste gases, and if they are allowed to accumulate they have a toxic effect on the organism. Look at the shell of an uncooked egg through your lens or, better still, hold a piece of shell from your breakfast egg up to a light. You will see numerous small openings, or pores. It is these openings, or pores, which provide for the entrance of air and the escape of the poisonous gases.

Speaking of the breakfast egg calls to mind our breakfast cup of coffee. Spread a little ground coffee and a little instant coffee on a piece of white paper and look at them with your lens. You will find that they differ markedly in appearance. The ground coffee will appear as shown in *Figure 2*. The instant coffee will appear as tiny brown beads or tiny brown bubbles (*Figure 3*). Instant tea appears much like instant coffee, although the beads appear larger, or at least those I have examined do. Regular tea differs considerably in appearance since it is simply the dried leaves of the tea plant or, if obtained from a tea bag, pieces of the leaves which have been shredded (*Figure 4*).

In many families breakfast is followed by a cigarette. Here is another very commonplace article which few of us have ever troubled to examine closely. If a member of your family smokes cigarettes, inspect the tobacco. You will find it consists of very small pieces of the tobacco leaf, which you would naturally expect to find (*Figure 5*). Examine the filter, too, if the cigarette is provided with one. And while we are on the subject of cigarettes and smoking, view the head of a paper match and the ashes of either a cigarette or cigar. You will find that the ashes look like the gray incrustations we often find on rocks and which we will study in a later Adventure.

Dust is an accumulation of all sorts of debris. It frequently figures in mystery stories and also in real-life police investigations. Criminals have been detected and convicted by dust found on their clothing, but we are not interested in criminal detection; rather in the substances we can identify in some sweepings. Sweep up a little dust from the floor or elsewhere onto a piece of white paper. See how many substances you can recognize.

In many ways soil is as interesting as dust, for you never know what you may find in the

Figure 4
SHREDDED TEA LEAVES

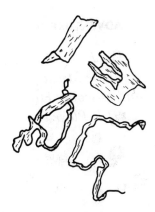

Figure 5
CIGARETTE TOBACCO

way of very small animals, seeds, and the remains of plants and animals. Also an examination of soil will enable you to determine what kind it is and whether it is suitable for a garden. Get an old spoon, go outdoors and dig up a spoonful of soil, bring it indoors, and spread it out on a piece of white paper. Good garden soil should contain a maximum of humus, which is formed by the partial decomposition of dead plants and animals or parts of them, and a minimum amount of sand and clay. Perhaps you may be able to identify some of the plants and animals from their remains (*Figure 6*). There are people who are experts in such matters.

ADVENTURE 2

*We Listen to
Some Music
and Discover How
It Is Played*

THE CHIRPING OF CRICKETS is a familiar sound on a summer's night, especially to those who live in the country. Only the males chirp. Why, I don't know. It was believed at one time that they play their fiddles to attract the females. But it has since been shown that the females pay no attention to the males' serenades. Someday we may know the reason. What we are primarily interested in is how the male crickets play. The best way to find out is to get one or two of them and observe them at close quarters. Incidentally, crickets make excellent pets and may be kept in a large jar or similar container with a little soil on the bottom. They can be fed bits of melon and other fruits, lettuce, and moist bread. A little bone meal should also be supplied to reduce cannibalism. If eggs are laid and you want to hatch them, sprinkle the soil with water as you would for plants. The female, by the way, can be distinguished from the male by the presence of a long, swordlike ovipositor, or egg-laying apparatus, extending from the end of her body.

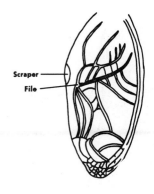

Figure 7
FOREWING OF MALE CRICKET

To return to our question of how a male cricket plays, observe that when he does so he lifts his wing covers at an angle of forty-five degrees and then rubs them together. Actually it isn't quite as simple as that. If you examine one of the wing covers with your lens, you will note that the venation is of a peculiar scroll pattern which probably serves as a framework for the purpose of making a sounding board of the wing membrane by stretching it out as a drumhead is stretched. Also note that near the base of the wing cover there is a heavy cross vein covered with transverse ridges called the file (*Figure 7*). Next find on the inner edge of the same wing near the base a hardened area. This area is called the scraper (*Figure 7*). When the cricket sounds his notes, he does so by drawing the scraper of the underwing cover against the file (*Figure 8*) of the overlapping one. We

Figure 8
SECTION OF FILE

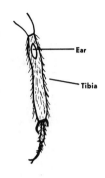

Figure 9
FRONT LEG OF CRICKET

can produce a similar sound by running a file along the edge of a tin can.

As the wing covers are excellent sounding boards and quiver when the note is made, the surrounding air is set into vibration, thus creating sound waves which can travel a considerable distance. An interesting sidelight in regard to this sounding device is that the cricket can alternate his use of the wing covers, that is, he can use first one wing cover as a scraper and the other as a file and then reverse them. In this way he can reduce the wear and tear and prevent them from being worn out.

Now there doesn't seem to be much sense in a cricket's being able to produce a sound unless he can hear it. If you look on the tibia of the front leg, you will note a small white disklike spot (*Figure 9*). This is the ear and is visible to the naked eye.

ADVENTURE 3

*We Give Seeds
More Than
a Passing Glance*

WE ACCEPT SEEDS for what they are and give little thought to them. Yet if we were to look at them more closely, especially with our lens, we would be amazed at their infinite diversity. They are as variable as the flowers that produce them and some are equally as beautiful.

Although they are typically more or less globular or oval in shape (*Figure 10*), there

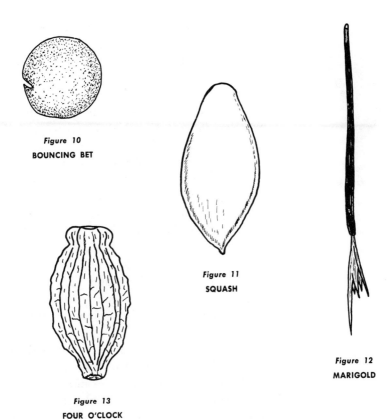

Figure 10
BOUNCING BET

Figure 11
SQUASH

Figure 12
MARIGOLD

Figure 13
FOUR O'CLOCK

are seeds that are extremely thin and flat
(*Figure 11*) or greatly elongated (*Figure 12*).
Seeds, too, may be smooth or wrinkled or
pitted or angled or furrowed (*Figure 13*).
There are seeds that are twisted or coiled

Figure 14
MOONSEED

(*Figure 14*) or otherwise irregularly distorted (*Figure 15*). Then there are seeds that are more or less covered with hairs or supplied with broad and extremely delicate membranous wings to make them wind-borne. In size the variations are equally pronounced. Some seeds are as fine as dust; others several inches in diameter; and, of course, there are seeds that represent all the gradations in between. But it is in the variety of color and color patterns that they show the most conspicuous external differentiation. I daresay we can find them matching every known color, from shining jet black through the gamut of blue, red, yellow, and other bright tints to the less striking and more somber brown and gray, to say nothing of the manifold designs produced by a blending of these colors.

Colors, needless to say, are not without some purpose. Seeds that are scattered by wind and water are, for the most part, inconspicuously or neutrally colored, but the bright and showy ones are designed to appeal to animal agents of dissemination. Although we may find the numberless variations somewhat surprising, what is even more surprising is that such an infinite variety should be produced under conditions that appear to be more or less uniform and constant. What may also seem incongruous is that plants that may appear superficially similar often produce seeds that are strikingly different, or that plants that are wholly unlike often produce seeds that are very much alike. Generally seeds are so characteristic that they serve as useful agents in classification, in some cases being so characteristically differentiated as to be an infallible clue to the identity of the plant that produced them.

A seed is botanically a ripened ovule and consists of an embryo plant and its protective covering or coat. The unripened ovule is a small structure in the ovary of a flower and may readily be seen by cutting the ovary open with a razor blade or pocketknife. In most cases you will find many ovules. The ovule contains an egg cell, and when this egg cell has been fertilized by a sperm cell, the ovule undergoes a number of changes and eventually develops into a seed. The sperm cell is contained in the pollen grain and must be transferred to the stigma of the pistil by some agent as the wind or an insect or by water or even by artificial means. Once the sperm cell has come in contact with the stigma, it makes its way down the pistil until it locates the egg, which it enters.

Obviously the embryo, which is a living plant whose growth has been temporarily suspended, is the most important part of the seed. Food, as a source of energy for the em-

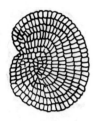

Figure 16
BABY'S BREATH

Figure 17
SPIDERWORT

bryo plant until it has developed to the stage where it can manufacture its own food, is stored within the seed. Long ago man discovered that he could make use of this reserve food for his own use. The seeds of wheat and rice are today the principal items of diet for millions of human beings, and countless others consume daily large quantities of such seeds as those of corn and barley, oats and rye. Beans and peas, which are also seeds, are eaten extensively. In addition to their value as food, man has found other uses for them. I might mention cottonseed oil, linseed oil, and coconut oil, which are used in the manufacture of substitutes for butter and lard, soap, and a variety of other products.

Although seeds exhibit a great diversity of surface markings (*Figure 16*) and configurations (*Figure 17*), they all agree in showing a minute pore or pit and a scar called the hilum. The pore or pit marks the position of the micropyle, an opening in the ovule through which the sperm cell entered on its way to the egg cell, and the hilum marks the place where the ovule was attached to the ovary. You should be able to find both of these structures with your hand lens (*Figure 18*).

Although seeds are more readily available during the summer and early fall, when they may be obtained from almost any plant outdoors, you should have no trouble in getting enough of them during the winter to observe the many variations I have mentioned. Your neighborhood hardware store may have some left from the preceding spring, and I would suggest you visit a local nursery. You should even be able to find some on your pantry shelves, for many seeds are used in cooking. As you examine different seeds, you will very likely begin to wonder how nature could design so many—I did when I first became interested in them. Perhaps it may also occur to you to make a seed collection. It is less expensive than collecting coins or postage stamps, and you should have a great deal of fun doing so.

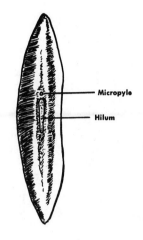

Figure 18
KIDNEY BEAN

SNAILS BELONG to a group of animals called the Mollusca. The word Mollusca is derived from the Latin *mollis,* which means "soft." Hence the group includes such soft-bodied animals as the snail, clam, oyster, squid, and octopus. All these animals have one thing in common—a shell. The shell may be a very simple and drab affair, or it may be highly sculptured and beautiful—to wit, some sea shells. It may also be in one piece, as in the snail, or it may consist of two parts, or valves, as in the clam. The shell of the land snail,

ADVENTURE 4

We Become Better Acquainted with the Snail

which we often find in our gardens, is a spiral cone made from a substance secreted by certain cells and that hardens on exposure to the air. The snail's soft body is twisted and coiled like the shell and extends into the apex, but usually does not completely fill the shell to the tip.

A snail may seem such an insignificant sort of animal and its actions may not seem to bear watching, but I think you will be in for a surprise if you find one and observe its behavior through your lens. In this instance a reading glass will prove to be of greater advantage than a pocket magnifier. Place the snail in a tumbler and watch it climb up the glass sides. As you do so you will find that the snail's foot is one of the most wonderful means of locomotion ever devised by nature. Observe how the foot stretches out and holds on, then contracts, and then again stretches out. All this is accomplished by muscles. Observe, too, how a slime gland at the anterior end of the foot deposits a film of mucus on which the animal travels. It lays down a sidewalk, as it were, ahead of itself, and this sidewalk is always the same whether the path is rough or smooth, uphill or downhill.

Although the shell provides the snail with a maximum amount of protection, it would seem to be something of a disadvantage to carry it around wherever it goes. Yet in spite

Figure 19
GARDEN SNAIL

of its cumbersome burden the little animal gets about remarkably well even though it will never set any speed records. Watch it for a while and you will discover that its pace is always about the same. It may be two inches per minute, ten feet per hour, or two hundred and forty feet per day if the animal keeps constantly on the move. It also appears to progress forward without any apparent muscular effort.

We frequently see on television and at the circus acrobatic stunts performed by contortionists. I doubt very much if these performers are any more loose-jointed than the snail. Watch the snail retire within its house. First it folds its foot lengthwise and then gradually withdraws it into the shell, the end on which the head is located first and then the hind end. Conversely, when the animal emerges, the hind end comes out first, and then the head and "horns." The "horns," of course, are not horns at all but tentacles (*Figure 19*). There are two pairs of tentacles (pond snails have only one pair, as you will discover should you find one), and both pairs are provided with little round, knoblike tips. On the longer pair the tips serve as eyes; on the shorter pair it is believed they function as organs of smell. It is said that a snail can detect food as far away as twenty inches.

You can determine this for yourself if you get a piece of apple or other soft food and place it at various distances. Observe how the animal uses its eyes to explore its surroundings and what happens if you place an object too close to it. Once it has located the piece of apple or fruit, you will find that it won't be long before it has made a good-sized hole in it. You will also observe that its table manners could be improved upon. It is a hopeless slobberer. The mouth is located directly below the tentacles and is furnished with one or more chitinous jaws and a long, ribbonlike tongue (the radula) that is covered with horny teeth. The snail uses its tongue as a rasp to file the surfaces of leaves or other food. The teeth vary in number, form, size, and arrangement in the different species of snails and are of considerable value in classification. If you want to examine these teeth more closely, you will need a microscope.

Before you return the snail to its natural environment, examine the skin with your pocket magnifier. It will remind you of an alligator's skin—rough and divided into plates with a surface like pebbled leather.

THE RUSTING OF IRON is a common occurrence, and we see evidence of it everywhere. Few of us have not sustained some loss or damage through rust, and perhaps a few of us have had the painful experience of having stepped on a rusty nail. The tendency of iron to rust is its most unfavorable property, and millions of dollars are spent annually to fight this enemy who, silently and unseen, is constantly bent on destruction.

You are taught in school that rusting is due to the action of oxygen in the air on the iron, which results in the formation of a reddish-brown substance called iron oxide. Actually it is not quite so simple. Furthermore, iron is not the only metal that can "rust." Most metals, when exposed to the air, are attacked by the elements and compounds present in the atmosphere. The phenomenon is generally known as corrosion; when applied to iron it is called rusting.

Examine a new and clean nail and note its appearance. Now wet it and leave it outdoors for a few days or until you observe brown spots on it. Look at these brown spots through your lens and you will find that they appear as incrustations that you can break off into small pieces with your fingernail. Next examine a really rusty nail—one that has been exposed to the air for a long time and is completely covered with rust. You will

We Inquire into the Nature of Rusting

Figure 20

NAIL COVERED WITH IRON OXIDE

find that it will have the appearance of a tree trunk that is covered with a reddish-brown flaky bark (*Figure 20*). The flakes come off easily, as they might off a real tree, if you scrape them with your fingernail or a pocket-knife. If you scrape enough off you will eventually expose the iron as you would expose the wood of the tree if you removed all the bark. Here the analogy ends, of course, since the bark serves as a protective covering for the wood, whereas the reddish rust has no protective value. Quite the contrary, for as it gradually flakes off through the action of rain and wind, the exposed iron in turn rusts until eventually the iron nail has completely disintegrated, or, more accurately, been converted into iron oxide.

In regard to this rusting of iron we should note two interesting facts. One is that pure iron will not rust and secondly that iron will rust only in the presence of water. Why is this? Both are explained by the electrochemical nature of the rusting process.

You are doubtless familiar with the electric cell. An electric cell, as you may recall, consists of two dissimilar metals or of a metal and carbon placed in a solution of an electrolyte. An electrolyte is a substance that, when dissolved in water, will conduct an electric current. The electric cell was invented, or perhaps it is better to say that the principle involved was discovered, by an Italian scientist, Alessandro Volta, over a hundred years ago. In the simple electric cell, known as the voltaic cell, a strip of zinc and a rod of carbon are placed in a jar of sulphuric acid. When the two are connected by a piece of copper wire, an electric current flows. It all has to do with electrons and ion exchange. Chemical energy is converted into electrical energy, and a substance, zinc sulphate, is formed.

Now a piece of iron, such as the nail, is usually not pure, but contains carbon, and when wet has all the essentials for an electric cell, since the water contains dissolved carbon dioxide, which forms carbonic acid with the water and is therefore an electrolyte. Under these conditions a similar reaction occurs as in the case of the zinc and carbon. A compound called iron bicarbonate is first formed and this is converted by the oxygen in the air into the familiar rust, or iron oxide.

Obviously all we need do to keep iron from rusting is to keep it dry, which is not too easily accomplished. That is why we cover iron girders and other forms of structural iron with paint and cover our tools and garden implements with grease or oil when not in use. Any substance that is impervious to air and water will do. Certain metals, as zinc, cadmium, and tin, are more resistant to rusting than iron and are often used as a coating.

The iron is dipped into the melted metal and a thin layer of it adheres to the iron. Iron thus coated is called galvanized iron. Another method of attacking this age-old problem of rusting is to alloy iron with other metals. An alloy is merely a mixture of two or more metals. Stainless steel, for instance, which is useful in building streamlined trains, for metal trim on buildings and automobiles, and for kitchenware, is a mixture of chromium, nickle, and iron.

ADVENTURE 6

*We Meet
the Insect Brownies*

THE INSECT BROWNIES are very small insects and are more appropriately known, at least to entomologists, as tree hoppers. They belong to the family of insects called the Membracidae and are very well named, since most of them live on trees and hop vigorously when disturbed. Not all of them, however, live on trees; some live on bushes and still others on grasses and other herbaceous plants.

If these insects are more correctly known as tree hoppers, why are they also called insect brownies? To answer this question, you first have to know what brownies are. In folklore they are believed to be good-natured goblins who are supposed to do various household chores by night. They have been pictured as whimsical little people with quaint, if not grotesque, faces. If you can picture in your mind these little imaginary people and then look a few of the tree hoppers full in the face, I think you will see the reason for calling them insect brownies.

A well-known entomologist once remarked that "Nature must have been in a joking mood when tree hoppers were developed." But I am not so sure that she was in a joking mood; on the contrary, I think she was quite serious when she designed these little insects, for their grotesque and bizarre appearance is not without value. They appear so much like spines and other plant structures in shape or form that they are not readily seen and thus escape detection by their enemies. The tree hoppers provide us with innumerable examples of what we call protective resemblance. I might mention just one—the common little tree hopper of the bittersweet. Its thornlike process resembles a thorn so closely that the insect can be distinguished from a real thorn only with difficulty.

How and where can we obtain these insects? You need an insect net, which you can make yourself or buy for a nominal sum, and a killing jar. The latter is merely a bottle with a screw cover with a piece of cotton attached to it so that the cotton will hang downward in the bottle. The killing jar serves as a lethal chamber, and in order for it to function all we need do is to soak the cotton in a fluid that will evaporate quickly. Carbon tetrachloride, which is used as a cleaning fluid and which can be purchased at a drugstore, will do nicely. It is not inflammable like alcohol or some other fluids we could use, but since it will kill the insects it is best not to inhale too much of it.

The best way to get tree hoppers is to walk through the grass of a field and swish the insect net back and forth through the grass or the wild flowers growing there. Do not swish your net among the branches of a shrub or tree, as it is very apt to get caught in them and tear. When you have passed your net through the grass a few times, examine it. You should find a large number of various insects crawling about in it. Now remove the cover from the killing jar and empty the contents of the net into the bottle, then replace the cover and wait a few moments until the fumes of the carbon tetrachloride have done their work. When all the insects are dead, remove the cover and shake the insects out onto a piece of paper or into a cardboard box where you can pick them over for tree hoppers. A pair of forceps or tweezers, such as you can get at the five-and-ten-cent store, will facilitate your handling the insects and will help you in holding them up when you examine them.

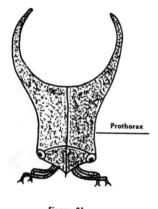

Prothorax

Figure 21
TREE HOPPER

As you view the tree hoppers through your lens, you will observe that the prothorax, which is the first segment of the thorax, the one next to the head, has been prolonged upward or backward or sideways according to the species you are viewing. It is this structure that nature has modified to produce the many strange and grotesque forms found among these insects (*Figure 21*).

Besides catching the tree hoppers with your net you might look over the twigs of various trees and shrubs and when you find them, which is not an easy thing to do, you can pick them off with your fingers or knock them into your killing jar. A common species you should have no trouble finding is the two-marked tree hopper (*Figure 22*). This species is very abundant on trees, shrubs, and vines and is gregarious, both adults and the immature forms being found clustered together. A good place to look is the bittersweet, where they are often found. If you find them, observe that no matter how the vine twists and turns they rest with their heads always toward the top. Can you suggest a reason for this? All tree hoppers suck the sap or juice of plants, and if they sit in this manner the sap can more easily flow down their throats.

Although tree hoppers suck plant juices, they do not occur in sufficient numbers to be of any economic importance. Sometimes the

Figure 22
TWO-MARKED TREE HOPPER

females of certain species injure young trees by laying their eggs in the bark of the smaller branches and in the buds and stems. The buffalo tree hopper is probably the most injurious, often causing considerable damage to young orchard trees and to nursery stock. It is grass green in color and somewhat triangular in shape with a characteristic two-horned enlargement at the front (*Figure 23*).

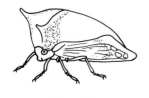

Figure 23
BUFFALO TREE HOPPER

ADVENTURE 7

We Visit Fairyland

LICHENS are of common occurrence except in the cities, where they do not seem to be able to grow because of the smoke and gases that pollute the air. We find them almost everywhere, and yet, in spite of their abundance, few people know what they are. Sometimes I wonder why it is that we so often fail to take more of an interest in things we see every day. How often have you observed the gray embroidery on a rock in a pasture, the yellow rosette on the trunk of a tree by the wayside, or the red coral on the decaying log or stump in the woods and given them only a passing glance? Perhaps they seem unimportant and therefore do not warrant our attention. But they are important, as we shall see.

Lichens are something of an oddity. They are not actually plants in the strictest meaning of the word, but a closely knit relationship of two entirely dissimilar plants living together for mutual benefit, a sort of partnership that biologists call mutualism. The two plants are an alga and a fungus. The alga is a relative of the simple green plants that are found on damp stones or on the shady sides of houses and trees. The fungus is a relative of the mushrooms that appear magically in our gardens after a heavy rain and the molds that so often appear on our foodstuffs, such as bread and jellies and cheese. The fungus has lost the ability, if it ever did have it, of manufacturing its own food, but instead has acquired the power of absorbing large quantities of water. If exposed to dry air the alga will perish, but when kept moist is capable of taking various elements from the air and converting them into food. So it is the function of the fungus to provide the partnership with water, and the alga to furnish the food.

Though the partnership may seem a strange one, it is a most successful one, for lichens can exist where no other plants can grow—on a bare alpine peak, in the arctic wastes, in a tropical desert. They need no soil —a bare rock will do or any kind of surface on which they can obtain a foothold. Because of their ability to live in such inhospitable places it would appear that they must be rather remarkable, as indeed they are. The mechanical contrivances that permit them to survive under what appears to be the most precarious of conditions have a strong appeal to the physicist, and the chemical processes that take place within them are of no less interest to the chemist, for, among other things, they secrete powerful acids that etch the rocks and break them up, thereby providing needed minerals for their own survival. The biologist regards the lichens with even greater respect because they are able to create soil in which other plants can grow. They represent the pioneer stage in a series of stages called ecological succession, a term given to the transition of a barren area into the climax forest through the intervening steps of a small pool, then a larger pond, followed by the swamp and marsh, and then the meadow and field. You will learn more about this when you study biology or, more specifically, that phase of biology called ecology.

Apart from their primary purpose of converting inhospitable waste ground into a soil suitable for other plants to grow in, some species also serve as food for various animals, such as the reindeer and caribou. Perhaps you have heard of reindeer moss, which is a lichen and not a moss. Not to be outdone by the animals, man has also made use of lichens as food. The people in Sweden at one time made a bread from one of them, and another species was once used in a Siberian monastery for a beer. The manna of the Israelites is supposed to have been a lichen. Drugs as well as various dyes have been obtained from certain species. The litmus we use in our chemical laboratories is obtained from a lichen.

But I think we have talked enough about the lichens. Let us go outdoors and look at them. Where shall we go? To some neglected pasture? To the woods? It doesn't matter. Wherever we turn, whether it is the marsh, the shore of a pond, the bank of a river, the roadside, we find them decorating trees, stumps, fallen logs, fence rails, rocks, almost any surface that will provide them with a foothold. And how may we recognize them? Almost any flat or ruffled and rootless growth of almost any color is likely to be a lichen, particularly if it bears flattened dish-shaped or saucer-shaped colored disks or cushions or if it branches like a coral or if it hangs like fringes from the branches of a tree. Best of all, we can find them at any time of the year, though they are at their best in spring and fall or even in the winter, for they like moisture and in the dry atmosphere of summer tend to dry out. In the summer, too, many of them are hidden by the foliage and other leafy vegetation and sometimes are rather difficult to find.

The first lichen to attract our attention will

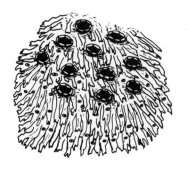

Figure 24
GRAY STAR LICHEN

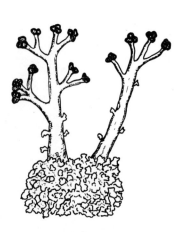

Figure 25
SCARLET CRESTED CLADONIA

Figure 26
GOBLET LICHEN

probably be the gray star lichen since it is fairly common on trees and rocks. It is a small but rather conspicuous silvery-gray or slate-gray rosette (*Figure 24*). Let us look closely at it with our hand lens and we will find small, flat disks, dark brown or black or frosted pale gray, with pale gray rims that may be smooth, toothed, or broken (*Figure 24*). The flat disks are the fruiting structures in which spores are produced, which perform the same function as the seeds of the higher plants.

As we look about we observe on the ground a coral-like growth with small red knobs. We view it with our lens and discover a most pleasing color contrast as we compare the frosted green branches and the little red tips. This lichen is the scarlet crested cladonia (*Figure 25*), sometimes called British Soldiers. It is a very common species throughout the Eastern United States, occurring on the ground, on tree bark, on fallen and decaying logs, and sometimes on stones. The little red knobs or cushions are the fruiting structures.

We continue to examine various lichens as we find them, and as we peer at them through our lens we become breathless at the unexpected beauty as revealed by the glass. And this is what I meant by heading this Adventure as a visit to Fairyland. Minute candelabra will appear as if by magic, and you will see tiny goblets that may have served the potter as models for his art (*Figure 26*). Examine the unkempt and rather dirty incrustations on the surface of a rock and you may well wonder if some ancient sculptor did not find inspiration in the beautiful designs traced by them. The intricate tracery that many of the lichens have embroidered on a bare and rather forbidding surface are no less remarkable than those you will find in the ornamentation of some marble temple. But I will let you discover all this for yourself.

As you become better acquainted with the lichens, I think you will become fascinated, too, with the many curious names that have been given to them. Old Man's Beard, the Dog Peltigera, the Crumpled Bat's Wing, and the Mustard Seed are only a few. They are all well named, too, as you will observe when you find them. The most interesting of all the lichens is, perhaps, the Rock Tripe. With every change in humidity the lichen curls and uncurls, writhes and twists, alternately covering the rock on which it grows with a green and black coating.

Once you have become interested in these odd plants, you may want to build up a collection. They keep well, for the most part, and even when dry may be made fresh looking by adding a little water. All you need is a knife and a hammer and a cold chisel.

Lichens growing on trees or logs are easily removed with a knife and those found on the ground and in rotton wood may simply be lifted up. The ones that grow on rocks present a more difficult problem, and here is where you need the hammer and chisel. At first it may seem almost impossible to separate them from the rocks, but with a little patience you will soon learn how to chip away fragments of even the hardest stone.

WE HAVE ALL HANDLED FEATHERS at some time but how many have looked at them closely or know how cleverly they are put together. There are several kinds of feathers, which vary somewhat in structure according to their function and position on the bird's body, but basically they are all the same. A typical feather is the contour feather. Contour feathers are the prevailing feathers. They are light in weight and provide a durable protective covering. They also serve as implements of flight. Equally important, they help to maintain the bird's body temperature. Air is an extremely effective insulating material and feathers are full of dead-air spaces. Perhaps you have observed birds fluffing out their feathers on a cold wintry day. This fluffing out, made possible by special muscles

ADVENTURE 8

We Examine a Feather

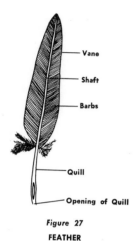

Figure 27
FEATHER

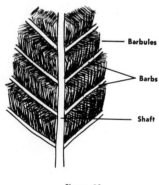

Figure 28
SECTION OF FEATHER

in the skin, increases the depth of insulating material by adding to the air spaces within the feathery layers. Conversely, on warm days the birds hold their feathers close to the body to allow some of the body heat to escape.

Feathers are easy to obtain, and you should have no difficulty finding one. Better get a contour feather, since this is the typical feather and best serves our purpose. The first thing you will probably notice about it is that it bears a superficial resemblance to a leaf (*Figure 27*) with its quill (petiole), shaft (midrib), and expanded portion, or vane or web (blade). But here the resemblance ends. Now examine the base of the shaft or quill and you will find it hollow, with a minute opening at one end. This opening is where the blood vessels entered the growing feather. Then note that the remainder of the shaft is solid and that the web, or vane, on each side is comparatively stiff and firm except where it was covered by the overlapping of other feathers where it is soft and downy.

Next hold the feather up to a bright light and look at a section of the vane through your hand lens. You will find that what appears at first to be a continuous leaflike surface is broken up into a series of barbs that are arranged on either side of the main shaft (*Figure 28*). Observe that they are set on a slight angle and more or less overlap at their edges. These barbs, in turn, are provided with innumerable little branches, called barbules, that overlap and interlock with the barbules of adjoining barbs (*Figure 28*). If your lens is of a high enough magnification (although you may need a microscope), you will further observe that the barbules are furnished with two kinds of projections called barbicels and hooklets (*Figure 29*). These barbicels and hooklets function as an interlocking device that gives the feather its consistency and stiffness and makes it impervious to air and water. It provides, however, a limited sliding arrangement of the barbules that gives more or less flexibility to the feather. The interlocking parts can readily be pulled apart, as you can find out for yourself by separating the barbs of the feather, and they can as easily be slipped back into place by drawing them through closed fingers. Birds repair such damaged feathers by drawing them through the bill.

Figure 29
BARBICEL WITH HOOKLET

ADVENTURE 9

*We Learn
the Meaning of
the Word Catkin*

HEARING THE WORD "catkin" for the first time, you would suspect that it would have reference to the cat, and you would not be mistaken. The dictionary tells us that the word means "having some resemblance to a cat's tail." You have doubtless noticed in early spring countless tassels hanging from the twigs and branches of certain trees and shrubs. From their fancied resemblance to the cat's tail they were given the name "catkin," and though they are also known botanically as aments, they are today more generally called catkins. Actually they are flower clusters.

Flowers such as the rose and lily and tulip are borne singly at the end of a long flower stalk and are called single or solitary flowers. In most flowering plants the flowers are borne in groups or clusters. A group or cluster results from the branching of the main flower stalk and is known as an inflorescence. There are different kinds of inflorescences, as the raceme, spike, cyme, corymb, umbel and, of course, the catkin, depending on the manner in which the flowers are arranged.

The catkins of the speckled alder* are among the first to appear in early spring. This small tree, so named because its stems are sprinkled or speckled with numerous and conspicuous light gray spots that are actually breathing pores called lenticels, is a water-

---

* The speckled alder is a shrub of the northern states but a closely related species, the smooth alder, is widely distributed throughout the south. The two, which may often be found growing together where their ranges overlap, are very much alike in habit and the catkins of either may be examined since they are similar.

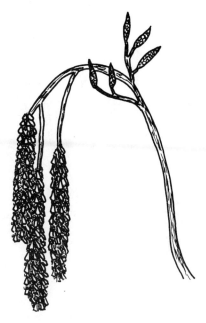

Figure 30
SPECKLED ALDER

loving plant and grows along the edges of ponds and streams and in swampy places. During the winter the unopened catkins are stiff and inflexible, but as the March sun climbs higher in the sky and the earth is warmed, the stiff fibers relax, the scales open, and the long, plumy tassels emerge to dance upon every passing breeze.

Let us examine one of these pendant tassels (*Figure 30*). As we look at it through our hand lens we find that it consists of brown and purple scales surmounting a central axis. We

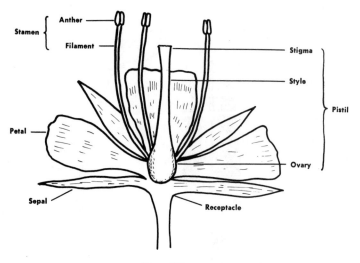

Stamen { Anther — Filament —

Petal —

Sepal —

Stigma — Style — Pistil Ovary —

Receptacle —

Figure 30A
DIAGRAM OF A SIMPLE FLOWER

further observe that the scales are set on short stalks and that beneath each scale are three flowers, each having a three-to-five lobed calyx cup and three-to five stamens whose anthers are covered with yellow pollen.

Let us pause at this point and recall our knowledge of botany. In spite of their striking external multiformity flowers are comparatively simple and uniform in their mode of construction. *Figure 30A* shows the diagram of a typical flower to which you can compare almost any blossom you have at hand. First we have the receptacle, which is the tip of the floral stem. Then we have the outer greenish leaves called sepals, which collectively are known as the calyx. Next we have the brightly colored leaves or petals, which collectively are known as the corolla. Within this corolla we have a whorl of appendages, the stamens. Each stamen consists of the filament, a slender cylindrical stalk bearing at its tip an enlarged rounded body, and of the anther, in which pollen grains, containing the male, or sperm, cells, are produced. Finally, within the whorl of stamens, and occupying the center of the flower, is the pistil, made up of modified leaves called carpels. The pistil consists of a cylindrical stalk called the style, with a rounded base, the ovary, and with a roughened area at the other end known as the stigma. The ovary contains a number of roundish bodies, within each of which, in a special sac, lies the female sex cell —the egg. When union of the egg cells and sperms has been effected—a process called fertilization—the roundish bodies, called ovules, develop into seeds.

Modifications and variations of such a typical flower frequently occur. As we look carefully at the flowers of the alder, we note that the pistil, an essential floral structure, is missing.

Now recalling our knowledge of botany,

we discover that the pistil, an essential floral structure, is missing. The absence of a pistil at first appears to be something of a puzzle until we examine one of the shorter erect catkins. Here we find that each of the fleshy scales, with which the catkin is provided, encloses two flowers, each having a pistil with a scarlet style. So there are two kinds of catkins on the alder, one having flowers with stamens only and the other with flowers having only pistils. In other words, we have what are known as staminate and pistillate catkins. Where both are found on the same tree, as in the alder, the tree is said to be monoecious.

Examining the flowers still further, we also observe the absence of petals. As the pollen grains are transferred from one flower to another by the wind, the petals would only be a hindrance and impede the wind from picking up the grains and acting as an effective agent of pollination. Here is an adaptation of distinct advantage to the plant.

Once pollination has been carried out, the pistils develop into small cones that resemble miniature pine cones. They consist of woody scales that protect the seeds formed beneath them. When the seeds are fully matured, the scales open and release the seeds, which are also scattered by the wind.

Next let us turn our attention to the pussy willow, whose furry catkins are a familiar

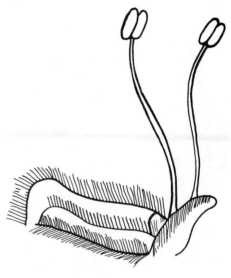

Figure 31
STAMINATE FLOWER OF
PUSSY WILLOW

sight in early spring throughout the Eastern and Central states. Unlike the alder, the pussy willow is dioecious, that is, the staminate and pistillate catkins occur on separate plants. Thus it will be necessary for us to locate two separate pussy willows, but this should not be difficult, since the plant is common and abundant. We can easily recognize the staminate plant because the catkins are profusely covered with yellow pollen. When we examine the flowers with our lens, we find that they each have two stamens (*Figure 31*).

Figure 32
PISTILLATE FLOWER OF
PUSSY WILLOW

Figure 33
STAMINATE FLOWER OF ASPEN

Now let us examine a pistillate catkin, which we can identify by the absence of the yellow pollen and by the very shape of the flowers themselves. When we do so we find that each flower has only a single pistil, with two more or less divided stigmas (*Figure 32*). If we keep the pistils under observation for a few days, we will find that they develop into conic-shaped capsules. These capsules contain the maturing seeds, and when the latter become fully developed the capsules will open. The seeds are furnished with long silky down that catches in the wind, an effective means that the pussy willow, in common with other plants, has evolved to ensure a wide distribution of its seeds.

The aspen is said to be the most widely distributed tree in North America. Most of us know it as the quaking aspen, because its leaves quiver or tremble in the slightest breeze. The catkins appear before the leaves, are furry, and show a touch of pink. The tree may be readily identified by its gray-green bark. Like the willow, the aspen is also dioecious. Note how the scales of the staminate flowers are deeply cut into three to four linear divisions and how they are fringed with long, soft gray hairs (*Figure 33*). The stamens number from six to twelve. The stigma is two-lobed (*Figure 34*), and the ovary is surrounded by a broad, oblique disk.

There is considerable variation in the flowers of the alder, willow, and aspen, even as there is in the more showy flowers. The variations may be small and seemingly insignificant, and yet they help us to identify and classify the plants. Of course, there are many other trees that bear catkins, among them being the birches, oaks, and hickories, and when they appear, examine them and note further variations. The staminate catkins of the black birch are fairly long, pendulous, and occur in clusters of threes; the pistillate catkins are much shorter, erect and solitary. The staminate catkins of the shagbark hickory are similar, but the pistillate ones occur on two- or five-flowered terminal spikes. Then in the white oak the staminate flowers are yellow, the pistillate red.

Figure 34
PISTILLATE FLOWER OF ASPEN

WE UNDERSTAND, of course, how insects and birds and airplanes can move through the air —it all has to do with air pressure and air flow and similar phenomena. Now has it ever occurred to you to examine a fly's wing with a hand lens? Probably not, so let us look at one and see what we find.

The best way to capture a fly without damaging it is with the killing jar, which we described in Adventure 6. Wait until a fly

ADVENTURE 10

We Study the Wings of Insects

alights on a flat surface, since it will then have the least chance of escaping, and then approach it stealthily with the uncovered jar and quickly place the jar over it. The startled insect will fly into the jar, and then you can replace the cover.

When the fly has inhaled enough of the poisonous fumes and shows no further signs of life, remove it from the bottle and examine one of the wings with your lens. It will appear as a piece of transparent parchment divided into a number of areas by thickened structures (*Figure 35*). Since a wing is a saclike fold of the body wall, it obviously must consist of two walls, but, looking at it, you would never suspect that such is the case, the two walls having been so closely fused together that the wing appears as a single membrane. The dual nature of the wing may be seen, however, along certain thickened lines where the two walls remain separated. These thickened lines are hollow and form the framework of the wing. They are called veins. Note how they are arranged. This arrangement is peculiar to the housefly, and in no other insect will you find them arranged in precisely the same way. Veins are known by certain terms according to their position. Thus veins are known as the costa, subcosta, radius, media, cubitus, and anal. The areas into which the veins divide the wing are called cells, and

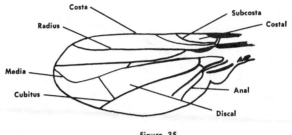

Figure 35
WING OF HOUSE FLY

these too are known by various terms, as dis-
cal, costal, etc., or they may be merely indicated by letters, as R_1, R_2, R_3, etc. The arrangement of the veins is known as venation
or neuration and serves as a means of classifying insects. As a matter of fact, the wings of
insects present such countless differences that
an expert can usually refer a detached wing
to its proper genus and often to its species
even though there are at present almost a
million known species.

With a few exceptions wings are usually
present in adult insects. They are more or less
triangular in shape, with three margins: front
(costal), outer (apical), and inner (anal); and
three angles: humeral (at the base of the
costa), apical (at the apex of the wing), and
anal (between outer and inner margins)
(*Figure 36*). Typically there are two pairs of
wings in an insect, although in some species

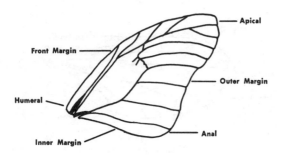

the females are wingless and in the vast group of true flies (Diptera) the second pair has been lost, having been replaced by knobbed, threadlike organs called halteres. The halteres appear to function as balancers, for the fly can no longer maintain its equilibrium if one of them is removed. See if you can locate them.

Next examine the wing of some other kind of insect—a butterfly, dragonfly, grasshopper, a beetle, a bee—better still, a number of them. As you do so, you will find that the front wings are variously modified, in some insects being more useful for protection than for flight. In grasshoppers (Orthoptera) the front wings are leathery and are called tegmina; in the beetles (Coleoptera) they are

Figure 37
WING OF MONARCH BUTTERFLY

Figure 38
WING OF COLORADO
POTATO BEETLE

usually horny and are known as elytra; and in the true bugs (Heteroptera) the base is thickened and the apex of the wing remains membranous, forming what is called a hemelytron. You will also observe, of course, that the veins in the wings of these various insects are differently arranged. The wing of the Monarch Butterfly is shown in *Figure 37,* and the wing of the common and destructive Colorado Potato Beetle is pictured in *Figure 38.*

I think you will agree that in flying an insect can make greater use of its wings if the fore and hind wings act in unison, much as the members of a boat's crew can attain greater efficiency with their oars if they all pull together. The synchronous action of the

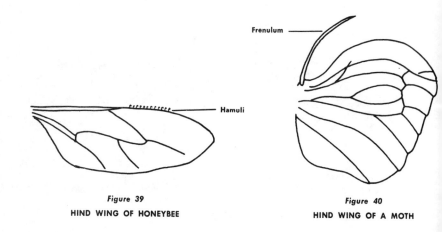

Figure 39
HIND WING OF HONEYBEE

Hamuli

Frenulum

Figure 40
HIND WING OF A MOTH

fore and hind wings is attained in insects by the fore wing's overlapping the hind wing, but in some species certain structures have been developed that fasten the two wings of each side together. Obtain a honeybee and examine the outer coastal margin of the hind wing (*Figure 39*). You will find a row of hooks, called hamuli, which fasten into a fold on the inner margin of the fore wing. Next examine the hind wing of a moth, where you will find at the humeral angle a strong, spine-like organ or a bunch of bristles called the frenulum, or little bridle. As a rule the frenulum of the female consists of several bristles; in the male it is a single, strong, spinelike organ (*Figure 40*). In the males of certain moths where the frenulum is highly devel-

oped, the fore wing has a membranous fold
for receiving the end of the frenulum.

WE DON'T HAVE TO WAIT for the circus to
come to town to see acrobats. The acrobats I
am thinking about we can find, figuratively,
in our own back yard or, put more accurately,
in the nearest pond. You may not find them
performing the death-defying feats that those
beneath the Big Top execute, but I think you
will find them just as interesting.

Just what are these acrobats? They are
small animals shaped like fleas, with arched
backs and narrow bodies, with climbing legs
on the thorax, and swimming and jumping
appendages on the abdomen. They belong to
a group called the Amphipoda and are really
accomplished water acrobats, as you will agree
when you have watched them for a time, for
they can climb and jump, swim or glide with
equal ease. As these acrobats are too small
really to be watched in their native habitat,
it is best to take a few of them home and
transfer them to an aquarium, where they
may be better observed.

There are several species of fresh-water
amphipods, but one of the most common and
abundant is Hyallela. In the spring it gathers
in large numbers in mats of the alga Spiro-

gyra to feed on the dead filaments, and this is a good time to collect it, although we can find it at almost any time of the year, even in winter. Hyallela does very well in an aquarium planted with some living water plants, as Elodea, Nitella, or Myriophyllum, and containing a few dead leaves. All of these can be obtained from almost any pond. The aquarium should be prepared and ready to receive its occupants. Hyallela may be taken from the pond by submerging a wide-mouthed bottle and letting the water flow in, or it may be collected with a pan or water net; in fact almost anything can be used that will hold water. Hyallela is about half an inch long and thus large enough to be seen with the naked eye. I have pictured it in *Figure 41* so that you will readily recognize it as it moves about in the water.

Because it is large enough to be seen with the naked eye, you can easily observe some of its habits, such as feeding and mating, without the use of your hand lens. But one of the most interesting phases of its behavior, for which you will need your lens to observe properly, is when it casts off its skin. Hyallela is a distant cousin of the lobster, crab, and crayfish, and if you know your zoology you know that these animals are crustaceans. The word "crustacean" is derived from the Latin *crusta*, which means "crust" or "shell" and

Figure 41
HYALLELA

refers to the hard outside covering possessed by these animals. This hard outer covering is made largely of a hard, inelastic material called chitin. Since this material cannot stretch, these animals periodically reach a point where growth can no longer take place beneath the hard covering. So it must be discarded. The casting off of this outer covering is called molting and is repeated a number of times, depending on the species, until full growth is attained. The molting process, which is in itself interesting to watch, can very well be observed in the case of Hyallela simply because it occurs so slowly. I don't want to describe it—I would rather have you watch it yourself and see how it takes place.

THE STUDY OF FLOWERS can be made highly absorbing because of their great diversity. Let us, for instance, examine the dandelion with our hand lens. Its appearance when viewed through the glass will be quite unlike what you saw with your naked eye. You will find that instead of being a single flower, which many suppose it to be, it is composed of many small flowers, and if you were to count them you would find that there would be somewhere between 150 and 200 of them. Each one of them is a perfect flower or floret;

ADVENTURE 12

We Go Botanizing

that is, each has both stamens and a pistil, but with a corolla consisting of a tube and a ray upon one side only. This corolla is straplike, with five teeth at the apex (*Figure 42*).

Once upon a time, this flower may have been a five-petaled blossom, for the five teeth at the top and the five lines descending from them would seem to indicate that once-distinct parts had been welded together to form a more showy and suitable corolla. Next see if you can find the five anthers that form a tube from which the pistil extends with its two-lobed stigma. You will note as you examine several of the florets that they may all be in various stages of development. The florets in the outer row of the dandelion head blossom first. After a corolla has opened, there first appears the anther tube, and then later the pistil, which gradually rises out of the anther tube and extends above it, when the stigma lobes quirl back.

Next let us examine the white clover. What appears at a casual glance to be a single flower is composed of a number of small flowers or florets. Each floret has a tubular calyx with five delicate points and a little stalk, and the corolla of five petals, which are very unequal, reminds us of the sweet pea (*Figure 43*). The superior petal, known as the standard or banner, more or less completely encloses the two lateral ones, and the two lower ones are more

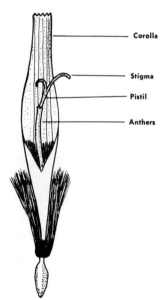

Corolla

Stigma

Pistil

Anthers

Figure 42
DANDELION

or less united into what is known as the keel. There are ten stamens, nine of which are united and one is free (see if you can find them), and one pistil. Incidentally, both the dandelions and the clover represent the type of inflorescence (see Adventure 9) called the head, which can be defined as a dense cluster of sessile or nearly sessile flowers on a very short axis. (Sessile flowers are flowers that are attached directly to the main stem without having a stem or stalk of their own.) Such a dense cluster is obviously more showy than the small florets and therefore more effective in attracting insect visitors.

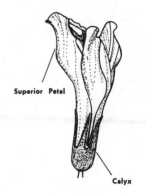

Figure 43
WHITE CLOVER

In early spring the bluets are a familiar sight in the fields and meadows of the Eastern and Central states. They are light blue, pale lilac, or nearly white with a yellowish center. Whatever the color, if we examine one of the flowers with our lens we observe that it is funnel-shaped with four pointed, petal-like oval lobes. An interesting feature of this plant is that it produces two kinds of flowers, which, however, are not found in the same patch. So if we want to examine both kinds we must look in different patches. If we select a flower from one patch, we may find that the two-lobed stigma extends above the opening of the corolla tube, and if we open the flower we will find four anthers fastened to the sides about halfway up (*Figure 44*). Now if we

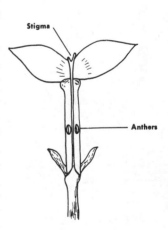

Figure 44
BLUET FORM A

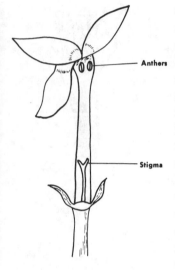

Figure 45
BLUET FORM B

move to another patch and select a flower from it, we find four anthers near the opening of the tube, but the stigma is not visible. If, however, we open the flower we find the stigma about halfway up the tube (*Figure 45*), in other words, just the reverse of what we found in the first flower. Thus, we have two kinds of flowers: Form A and Form B. The reason for the two kinds is, of course, to secure cross-pollination. An insect visiting Form A (*Figure 44*) gets its tongue dusted with pollen from the anthers at the middle of the tube. This pollen is brushed off by the stigma of Form B (*Figure 45*). Conversely, an insect visiting Form B gets the base of its tongue dusted with pollen, which is removed by the protruding stigma of Form A.

One of the more conspicuous wild flowers of summer is the wild carrot, also known as Queen Anne's Lace (*Figure 46*). The large white, circular, flat-topped clusters (known as umbels) are familiar in fields, along roadsides, and in waste places. When viewed with the naked eye the clusters appear to be a lacework of some beauty, but it is only when we examine them with our lens that we can appreciate their delicate structure and perfection of detail. One of the first things we notice is that the flowers are of unequal size, but each with five petals and five stamens and two styles. We also observe that what appeared to the naked

Figure 46
WILD CARROT

eye to be a single cluster is actually composed of a number of small clusters. A very odd feature of the cluster (I am now speaking of the entire cluster) is that at the very center there is a large floret with delicate, wine-colored petals. This floret, as you will note, is not a part of any of the smaller clusters but is entirely separate and is set upon its own isolated stalk. The presence of this striking floret in the very center of the wide, circular flower cluster is a mystery—I know of no one who has been able to account for it. Even-

Figure 47
GOLDENROD

Figure 47A
DISK FLOWER OF ASTER

tually the entire cluster dries up and resembles a bird's nest. We shall refer to it in a later Adventure.

In late summer and early fall the goldenrods dress the fields with their waving wands in a cloth of gold. Let us detach one of the flowering stems and look at it through our lens. What we find is a surprising row of tiny yellow goblets (*Figure 47*). The asters, too, are a familiar sight at this time of the year and to the eye appear as central yellow disks surrounded with an outer ring of what appear to be petals, variously colored in white or tints of blue, violet, or purple. If we were to examine any one of them with our lens, we would discover that the central disk is composed of many erect tubular blossoms that, yellow at first, change later to purple or brown with age. They are known as the disk flowers (*Figure 47A*). The so-called petals are elongated, strap-shaped blossoms known as the ray flowers (*Figure 47B*). Comparing them carefully, we find them unlike for the reason that the ray flowers are pistillate, that is, with pistils only, whereas the disk flowers are perfect, meaning that the disk flowers have both stamens and pistils—in other words, both male and female organs of reproduction. The ray flowers are female only.

The evolutionary changes that brought about the present floral arrangement in the asters—for they were not originally as they are today—make a most interesting story, but too long a one for this book. What we can say is that, as the flowers and insects developed side by side and each became more and more aware of each other's requirements, mutual adaptation followed. The flowers that offered the greatest benefit to the insects and advertised their wares most blatantly, and in turn employed their insect visitors to the fullest in distributing their pollen, were the most successful. This is what the asters, as well as other flowers, were able to do.

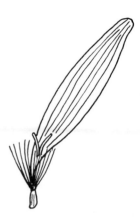

Figure 47B
RAY FLOWER OF ASTER

ADVENTURE 13

We Compare Insect Antennae

YOU HAVE DOUBTLESS read of how ants communicate with one another by means of their antennae, or feelers. Perhaps you have actually seen them do so.

Let us pick up the ant and examine its antennae closely with our lens. We find that it is composed of a number of segments joined together in a linear series and that its entire appearance is quite different from when viewed with the naked eye. Next let us count the many segments. Perhaps we may have to repeat our count several times before we are sure of the correct number.

The antennae of insects are commonly regarded as organs of touch. However, in the ant's antennae, segments eight through twelve have been modified for the purpose of detecting odor. By means of the twelfth segment the ant can detect the odor of any descendant of the same queen and thus be able to recognize the members of its own community wherever it may find them. The tenth segment enables the ant to recognize the odor of its own feet and thus be able to retrace its own steps. Lastly, the eighth and ninth segments provide the ant with the means and intelligence of caring for the young. If an ant should be deprived of these five end joints of its antennae, it has no further caste as a social ant and loses its standing in the community.

Now that we have found that the antennae of insects are composed of segments joined together in a linear series and that the segments may be variously modified to perform certain functions, let us examine the antennae of a few other species, and as we do so we will find that the antennae differ, not only in form, but, in some species, between the male and female. The stinkbugs are a

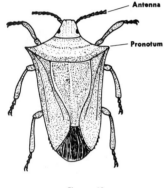

Figure 48
BROWN STINKBUG

group of fairly common insects abundant on various plants. The rather crude, if not vulgar, term that has been fastened on them is due to a fluid secreted through two openings on the lower surface of the thorax. Another name for them is shield bugs, because of the large scutellum, or shield-like area. If we look on tomato, eggplant, and related plants, we should have no trouble finding the brown stinkbug, also called the spined stinkbug. It is a medium-sized brown species with an angle on each side of the pronotum (*Figure 48*). Examining the antennae with our lens, we note that the segments are all of a nearly uniform size, giving the entire antennae a threadlike appearance. Scientists call this type of antennae filiform (*Figure 49*).

Next let us visit a pond or stream where we want to examine the antennae of a dragonfly. To do so we must take along our insect net (see Adventure 6). Dragonflies are not easy to capture, particularly some of the larger species, which are expert flyers. One of the common and abundant species is the white-tail, which is easy to recognize since the males are powdered with white, so let us concentrate on capturing one of these. When we finally do so and examine one of the antennae, we observe that the segments are successively smaller and smaller, the entire organ tapering to a point. In other words, the

Figure 49
FILIFORM

Figure 50
SETACEOUS

Figure 51
CLAVATE

antenna appears bristle-like, and here again the scientists have a word for it, setaceous (*Figure 50*).

Since we are outdoors with a butterfly net, we may as well next turn our attention to the monarch or milkweed butterfly. Most of us are acquainted with this rather large, ruddy-brown butterfly we see flying over fields and along roadsides and occasionally in our gardens during the summer months. Its caterpillars feed exclusively on the milkweed, hence its name. The monarch has antennae quite unlike those of either the stinkbug or dragonfly, as you will discover when you capture one and look at its antennae. You will note (*Figure 51*), that they

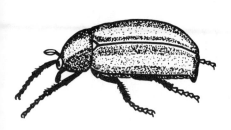

Figure 51A
JUNE BEETLE

Figure 52
LAMELLATE

are club-shaped (clavate), the segments becoming gradually broader so that the entire
structure has the appearance of a club.

Another insect whose antennae we should
also examine is the June beetle (*Figure
51A*). This is the large mahogany-brown
beetle that makes its appearance in May or
June and may often be found flying about
our porch lights at night. Sometimes it bangs
against our screens with a resounding noise
that is quite startling. You will find that the
segments that compose the tip or knob are
extended on one side into broad plates, forming a somewhat lamellated (plated) structure, whence the term "lamellate" for this
type of antennae (*Figure 52*). If you are not

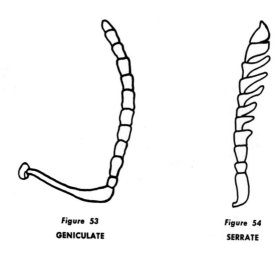

Figure 53
GENICULATE

Figure 54
SERRATE

too timorous about going after a bumblebee, you will find that the antennae of this insect are oddly shaped. All of the insects we have discussed so far may be examined without danger while alive, but it is inadvisable to examine a bumblebee in this fashion. It is best to capture one with a butterfly or insect net and then place it in a killing jar* until life has been extinguished, when it may be handled safely. You note that the antennae are bent abruptly at an angle like that of a bent knee. This type is called geniculate (*Figure 53*).

There are many other forms of antennae,

---

* See Adventure 6.

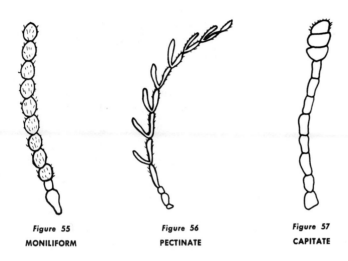

Figure 55
MONILIFORM

Figure 56
PECTINATE

Figure 57
CAPITATE

as you will discover by examining various insects: sawlike (serrate, *Figure 54*), in which the segments are triangular and project like the teeth of a saw; necklace-form (moniliform, *Figure 55*), in which the segments are more or less spherical, suggesting a string of beads; comblike (pectinate, *Figure 56*), in which the segments have long processes on one side, like the teeth of a comb; or in some species the antennae may have the last segment greatly enlarged, forming a large knob (capitate, *Figure 57*).

Finally, if you were to compare the antennae of the male and female cecropia moth or those of the male and female mosquito, you would find that those of the male cecropia are larger and more feathered than those of the female. The reason for this is that the male seeks out the female by means of the sense of smell and depends on his antennae to detect the odor given off by the female. In the case of the mosquito, the male uses his antennae to locate the female through the sense of hearing, the delicate fibrillae of the antennae (*Figure 58*) being sent into sympathetic vibration by the note of the female, much as our radio and television aerials pick out the waves sent out by the transmitting stations. Besides serving as organs of touch, smell, and hearing, antennae also function in some species, as in the water scavenger beetle, as respiratory organs. Some male insects use them in mating.

We may now ask how insects perceive the various stimuli that enable them to react and behave as they do. To learn how they do this, we need only to re-examine the antennae a bit more closely, and in some cases a microscope might be required, when we find that for the perception of sensory impressions the integument, or external covering, of the antennae has been further modified into cones (*Figure 59A*), peglike projections (*Figure 59B*), bristles or fine hairs (*Figures 59C and D*), plates (*Figure 59E*), and flask-shaped cavities and the like (*Figure*

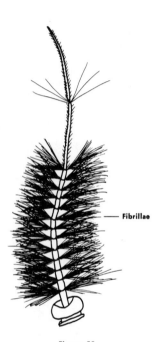

—— Fibrillae

Figure 58
ANTENNA OF MALE MOSQUITO

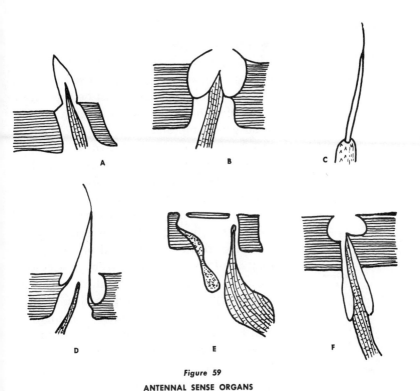

Figure 59
ANTENNAL SENSE ORGANS

59F). It is these adaptive structures that serve as sense organs and that respond to the stimuli of sound, smell, and touch. The subject is an exhaustive one and obviously we cannot go into detail here, but if you would like further information I would suggest that you consult any standard textbook on insect anatomy and physiology.

ADVENTURE 14

We See How
Ants Keep Clean

Figure 60
ANTENNA CLEANER OF ANT

IN OUR LAST ADVENTURE we learned that insects use their antennae to detect sound and odors, and for various other purposes. In order to function successfully it seems rather obvious that these organs must be kept clean. Ants, then, have a utilitarian reason for personal grooming, and as we have combs and brushes, so, too, do they have means of removing dirt and other debris from their bodies. Let us see what they are.

If you have not already observed ants in the act of cleaning their antennae, I would suggest that you get three or four of them and place them in some kind of a container that would serve as a sort of observation chamber. A large glass dish filled with earth and provided with a cover so that the ants cannot escape would do nicely. It might be well before watching them at their ablutions to examine first the front leg with your lens. You will note a curved, movable, comblike spur on the distal end of the tibia, and opposite it, on the base of the metatarsus, a concavity tipped with hairs (*Figure 60*). This is the antenna cleaner. In cleaning its antenna the ant, as you will observe, lifts its leg over the antenna and then draws the antenna through the space between the spur and hairs, which effectively act as a brush. A dirty brush is of little value, so after cleaning the antennae the ant proceeds to do the same with the

Figure 60A
ANT COMBING ANTENNAE

brush, licking it clean by passing it through
its mouth. The performance is interesting
and amusing to watch (*Figure 60A*).

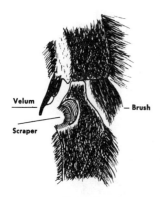

Figure 61
ANTENNA CLEANER OF HONEYBEE

Velum

Scraper

— Brush

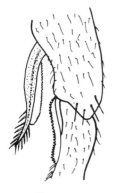

Figure 62
ANTENNA CLEANER OF
YELLOW JACKET

The honeybee is also provided with an antenna cleaner. If you obtain a bee (be sure to use your insect net and killing jar,* because you do not want to get stung, which can be a very painful experience) and examine the front leg with your lens, you will find a concavity, or semicircular scraper, on the tarsus (*Figure 61*). When the bee wishes to clean its antennae, it raises its leg and passes it over an antenna, which then slips into the scraper. The bee now bends its leg at the joint where the tibia and tarsus meet, and as the leg is bent, an appendage, called the velum, falls into place to complete a circular comb through which the antenna is drawn. The comb itself is cleaned by means of a brush of hairs on the front margin of the tibia (*Figure 61*).

A third insect also provided with a cleaning structure is the yellow jacket. The yellow jacket is a wasp, and you have doubtless often seen it, for it is quite common. There are a number of species of yellow jackets, but they are all very much alike, small in size and black and yellow in color. They make a nest of paper which most of them place in the ground, although a few species build the nest in a stump or under some object lying on the ground. If you examine the foreleg of one of these wasps (and I must caution you that

* See Adventure 6.

wasps can inflict a severe sting, so use your net and killing jar), you will find that its antenna cleaner is really a comb in every sense of the word and quite ornate at that (*Figure 62*).

MANY YEARS AGO Charles Darwin, whose book *On the Origin of Species* is a milestone in the history of biology, wrote another book, *The Formation of Vegetable Mold through the Action of Worms,* in which he shows how valuable the earthworm is to the farmer because of its underground activities. To most of us the earthworm seems of no possible use except as bait for catching fish, but actually it is among our best friends, for, unseen, it works day and night, harrowing and fertilizing the soil for our benefit. It burrows into the ground from twelve to eighteen inches and brings the subsoil to the surface. It also grinds the soil in its gizzard and turns it into a finer texture than we are able to do; it even fertilizes the soil by secreting lime that neutralizes the acids in it.

The earthworm is not only a mere tiller of the soil, it is also an agriculturist, for it plants fallen seeds by covering them with soil and cares for the growing plants by cultivating the soil around the roots. Furthermore, it enriches the soil by burying the bones of dead

ADVENTURE 15

We Find out how the Earthworm Moves

animals, shells, leaves, twigs, and other organic matter that, upon decaying, furnishes the necessary minerals to the plants. It even provides drainage by boring holes to carry off the surplus water, and by so doing also promotes aeration.

As you can see, the earthworm is not so useless after all. The changing character of the landscape and much of the beauty of our fields and forests can be attributed to the labors of this diminutive workman. The familiar mounds of black earth or castings that can often be seen on the ground are particles of soil swallowed in their burrows and brought to the surface. Since there may be as many as fifty thousand worms in an acre of ground, Darwin estimated that more than eighteen tons of earthy castings may be carried to the surface in a single year on one acre of ground, and in twenty years a layer three inches thick would be transferred from the subsoil to the surface. Then he goes on to say that "it may be doubted if there are any other animals which have played such an important part in the history of the world as these lowly organized creatures." That their work is of tremendous agricultural importance can hardly be disputed. Remember this the next time you impale one on a hook.

We are not particularly interested here in the agricultural activities of the earthworm,

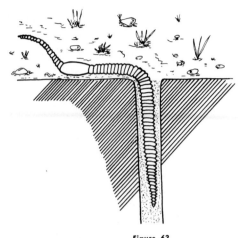

Figure 63
EARTHWORM IN ITS BURROW

but rather in the way it gets around. No doubt you have seen an earthworm wriggling over the ground, but have you ever wondered how it does so with what appears to be a relatively smooth body? It would seem that all the earthworm could accomplish by means of its wriggling movements would be merely to thrash about in one spot. Again, have you ever seen a robin tugging away at a protesting worm, or tried yourself to pull one out of its burrow and to your surprise found it was not an easy thing to do? You found it anchored there but did you ever wonder why it was so difficult to dislodge (*Figure 63*)? The explanation is a simple one. If you take hold of an earthworm and run your fingers along its sides or lower surface, you will find it rough to your touch. The effect is much the same as if you ran your finger over a stiff toothbrush.

In both instances the roughness is due to stiff bristles. Examine the earthworm with your lens and you will see these stiff bristles projecting from the body. There are four pairs of these bristles, or setae, as they are called, on every segment of the body except the first three and the last. (You will have noticed by this time that the body of the worm is composed of a linear series of segments, hence the animal is known as a segmented worm). The bristles protrude from small sacs in the body wall and can be extended or retracted by special muscles. If the earthworm wants to remain fixed in its burrow, all it has to do is to extend the bristles out beyond the body surface and into the sides of its burrow and it will be securely anchored, much as an anchor holds a ship in place. Of course you can dislodge an earthworm from its burrow by the use of superior force, but you will very likely injure it or even kill it.

The presence of these bristles also explains how the earthworm can move over the surface of the ground or in and out of its burrow, although as a rule it rarely leaves its burrow, because the worm, for some reason, cannot seem to find its way back once it has left. Watch the worm crawl over the ground and you will observe that it makes its way along by first extending the anterior part of its body, anchoring this part of the body by means of its bristles, and lastly drawing up the posterior part. The bristles on this part are then extended into the ground, those of the anterior part are retracted and the anterior part extended lengthwise over the ground. All this is accomplished by two sets of powerful muscles, one set running circularly around the body, the other lengthwise. You can see the movements of these muscles if you look closely. While you have the earthworm in your hand, look at one of the segments with your lens about part way between the pair of bristles on the side and the pair on the lower surface. You should find a small pore, or opening. This is the external opening of the excretory system and is called the nephridiopore. There is a pair of them on every segment except the first three and the last. Now look on the upper surface of the animal and you will observe a reddish-purple line. This is the main blood vessel, and you can see the pulsations as the blood flows through it. You will also note at the anterior end a fleshy lip called the prostomium. The prostomium is used to push food into the mouth. You can watch its actions through a reading glass if you place a worm in a glass dish containing some earth and give it small pieces of a lettuce or cabbage leaf.

ADVENTURE 16

We Discover that There Are Different Kinds of Hairs

HAVE YOU EVER GRASPED a petunia leaf and found it sticky or clammy to the touch? Did you ever wonder why? Look at the lower surface with your lens and you will find it covered with numerous fine hairs. Hold the leaf up to a bright light and the hairs seem to glisten. The tips are glandular and secrete a sticky material that reflects the light, making them sparkle or glitter. Touch a geranium leaf and you will find it sticky too, and for the same reason, as you will discover if you examine the lower surface. There are other plants that are similarly furnished with glandular hairs, as the tarweeds, tobacco, Chinese primrose, and pumpkin and squash and other members of the gourd family.

As a matter of fact, many plants are provided with hairs, but not all are sticky; to the touch they feel much like those on our own bodies. Hairs are outgrowths of the epidermal, or surface-layer, cells and may consist of only one cell (*Figure 64*), when the epidermal cell and hair are one and the same,

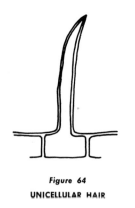

Figure 64
UNICELLULAR HAIR

or they may consist of many cells (*Figure 65*). In the latter instance the hair is a filament that decreases in size from the base to the apex. A glandular hair bears at the upper end a rounded head (*Figure 66*). Hairs entrap air, which reflects light and makes them appear white or nearly so.

In some plants the hairs may form only a slight downy covering, or they may form a woolly or feltlike mass. The leaves of the common mullein are so woolly that certain small insects, as the thrips, find a good winter retreat among them. The hairs form a dense network, and if you look closely at a single hair you will observe that it is much branched (*Figure 67*). The mullein is a very common and picturesque plant of rocky pastures, roadsides, and waste places and can easily be recognized by its long stem, which extends as high as six or seven feet. The large, rather succulent and velvety-appearing leaves seen at a first glance to be good eating, but if you have the courage to bite into one of them you will quickly find out why sheep and other grazing animals leave them alone. Hairs, then, are something of a protective device, although in some instances they may not be very effective. Hairs are also supposed to retard transpiration or to reduce water loss through evaporation. Research has shown that, although dead hairs may accomplish

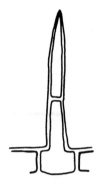

Figure 65
MULTICELLULAR HAIR

Figure 66
GLANDULAR HAIR

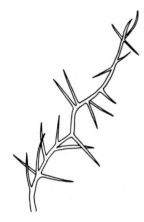

Figure 67
HAIR OF MULLEIN LEAF

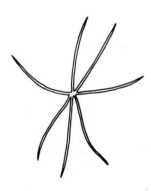

Figure 68
HAIR OF MALLOW

something in this respect, living hairs are useless for the purpose.

The pearly everlasting is another densely woolly plant found in old fields and along roadsides from summer to fall. If you are unacquainted with it, you may easily recognize it by its linear leaves and white tubular flowers in clusters at the summit of cottony stems, the stems as well as the leaves being profusely covered with hairs. Look at one of the leaves with your lens and you will find that it is covered with such a dense layer of what appears to be cotton fibers that it disguises all venation except the midrib.

If you find in someone's garden the plant variously called lamb's-ears, bunnie's-ears, or woolly woundwort, you will note that the plant appears entirely white due to the dense covering of hairs. Examine the hairs with your lens and you will find them to be smooth and silken, and when you rub them with your finger they will feel just like fur. Another garden plant you should locate, if possible, is the vervain mallow, or European mallow, because the hairs with which it is covered are star-shaped. Each hair consists of a short stalk from the upper end of which a number of branches radiate out at right angles like the points of a star (*Figure 68*).

The leaves of the bush clover, a common plant in pastures, thickets, and open woods, are provided with finely appressed hairs on the lower surface. In other words, the hairs lie close and flat to the surface, as shown in *Figure 69*. Note the bristles at the tip of the leaflets. In some plants, notably the thistle, the hairs have become stiff and bristle-like, and when viewed with the lens appear a most effective deterrent to animals. As you examine various leaves at random, you will find other variations, too, as in the oleaster (*Figure 70*) and buffalo berry, whose leaves bear shield-shaped hairs that consist of a single scalelike expansion at the end of a short stalk.

Figure 69
HAIRS OF BUSH CLOVER

Figure 70
HAIR OF OLEASTER

Aphids are sometimes called plant lice, but the word, though descriptive, is a misnomer, since they are not lice at all. Since they sometimes infest a plant in such numbers that you can hardly see anything else and because they are sucking insects, as are the lice, someone once thought the name appropriate and it has stuck with them ever since. They are somewhat flask-shaped in outline, with two large eyes set rather apart (*Figure 71*). Most aphids are green in color, but there are some species that are otherwise colored, and a few have the most bizarre and striking ornamentations.

Aphids are abundant and occur on almost

ADVENTURE 17

*We Spy
on the Aphids*

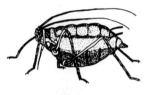

Figure 71
APHID

every kind of plant, so you should have no difficulty in locating a colony. They are visible to the naked eye but can be observed best with a lens. Note that they are in all stages of development and in various positions: some of them have their beaks in the tissues of the plant in the process of sucking the juices, with their hind legs high in the air and their antennae curved backward; others have their beaks tucked under their bodies, walking slowly about stiff-legged, perhaps looking for some likely spot in which to thrust their beaks; while others just sit quietly gazing out at the world with their large eyes. Sometimes there are so many clustered on a stem that those moving about must climb over the backs of the others, and the smaller ones are so tightly pressed between the larger ones that it seems as if they would be squeezed to death. These little insects may appear innocent enough, but they are actually very destructive to plant life, and if it were not for their enemies they would become a real menace.

You will note that all the aphids are wingless. They are all females, too. Now what is most interesting is that, without the aid of males, these females produce living young, which in turn, also being females, produce more young. This continues for generation after generation until the plant becomes so crowded that it cannot possibly support any more. What happens then? When the colony has reached such a size, winged females are produced that fly to another plant. Usually it is the same kind of plant, but in some species of aphids it may be a different kind of plant. In either case these winged females start another series of wingless generations. You can readily see why there are so many aphids. Even through a single female doesn't produce many young, the young are all females that in turn produce more females.

This sort of thing cannot continue forever, of course, especially when cold weather comes. As adults the aphids cannot survive the winter, but as they found out how to cope with overcrowding they also discovered how to solve the problem of low temperatures. When the first cold days of autumn herald the approach of winter, perfect winged males and females are produced. The males and females mate and the females lay their eggs in the crevices of bark or at the base of buds and branches. The eggs remain unhatched through the winter and in the following spring, or in midsummer, according to the species, hatch into young. These young establish themselves on a favorable plant and within a few days produce young that, of course, are females, and the cycle starts all over again. The young females that hatched from the eggs are known as "stem mothers" because they initiate the new colonies.

Another odd and interesting facet in the life history of the aphids is that during the successive generations a number of different forms may be produced in each species. In one species as many as twenty-one different forms have been noted. This makes the study of aphids rather confusing. Hence it is very likely that the four hundred or so aphids that have been described from the United States as distinct species may actually be forms of a smaller number of real species.

Aphids appear to be utterly defenseless and they are for the most part, but some of them can secrete a waxy substance in the face of an enemy and thus effect their escape. Most aphids also secrete a sweetish substance called honeydew, which has a particular appeal to bees, wasps, and ants. The bees and wasps take it where they can find it but some species of ants go to considerable lengths to care for the aphids, herding them as "cows" and protecting them against enemies, so that they always have a supply at hand. As you watch the aphids through your lens, you may see some ants stroking the aphids with their antennae until they respond to such caresses with a glistening drop of the fluid, which is immediately snatched up by the ants.

IN OUR LAST ADVENTURE we observed how the aphids obtain their food. They have, as we noted, a long beak which they insert into the tissues of plants and which is an effective piercing and sucking organ. We cannot see the sucking apparatus unless we dissect the insect, but it consists essentially of a sort of bulb which functions much like a medicine dropper. Unlike other groups of animals, whose mouth parts are more or less constant, those of the insects differ in the various orders and represent many interesting and highly adaptive modifications.

For instance, the mouth parts of the butter-fly form a tool which is effective for obtaining nectar, but is quite incapable of piercing plant tissue. It is basically a long tube called the proboscis (*Figure 72*), which is held ordinarily coiled beneath the insect's body, but at the time of feeding is uncoiled and extended into the nectary of the flower. You can observe the manner in which this is done by taking up a position near a flower and by means of a reading glass watch what happens when a butterfly alights.

All insects, of course, do not obtain their food from plant juices or nectaries; many of them feed directly on the plant tissues such as leaves, biting off small pieces and then chewing them much as we might eat an apple. Watch a grasshopper feed (and here again a

We Become Familiar with the Eating Habits of Insects

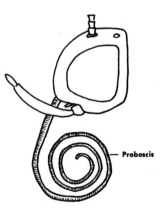

— Proboscis

Figure 72
MOUTH PARTS OF BUTTERFLY

reading glass is best) and you will observe the upper jaws, or mandibles, which look like a pair of nippers, cut out pieces of leaf or grass blade (*Figure 73*). Note, too, that the jaws move sideways instead of up and down, as they do in most animals provided with jaws. You will further remark that the grasshopper is provided with two pairs of appendages (not the antennae), with which it constantly taps the leaf as it eats. Called palpi, they are organs of touch and are used to test the leaf to make sure it is good to eat before the insect bites into it.

Some people seem to think that the grasshopper's face has a rather droll expression (*Figure 73*). It is a long face, not unlike that of a horse, and not particularly prepossessing, and yet it is not without a certain strength of character if we can read character into the face of an insect. As we watch it feed it seems to do so with a certain air of smugness and takes each bite as if it really enjoyed eating. Considering the damage grasshoppers inflict on our crops, they probably relish the gastronomic delights we provide them.

While you are watching the grasshopper dine, note the two large eyes, which you can hardly miss. Examine them closely and you will find that each is divided into a number of small divisions or areas that are commonly more or less hexagonal. Each of these areas

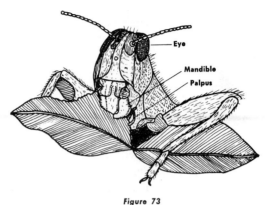

Figure 73
GRASSHOPPER FEEDING

is called a facet and is the outer surface of
a single eye, so what appears to be a single
large eye is actually composed of a number of
individual smaller eyes. These compound
eyes of the grasshopper (and other insects as
well) form what is known as a mosaic image.
The number of facets varies in different insects. There are four thousand of them in the
eye of the ordinary housefly, but this is a
small number compared to the seventeen
thousand of the swallowtail butterfly or the
twenty-seven thousand in a sphingid moth.

There are two general types of mouth
parts in insects, the sucking type, as in the
butterfly and aphid, and the biting type, as

Spoon

in the grasshopper. Now some insects have both kinds, as the honeybee, but these insects are essentially sucking species, the mandibles, which are the biting tools of the grasshopper, being modified for some other use. If you examine the mouth parts of the honeybee through your lens, you will observe that the mandibles (*Figure 73A*) are well-developed instruments for cutting and that the remaining mouth parts form a highly complex suctorial apparatus. Look also at the tongue and you will note that it terminates in a "spoon" and is clothed with hairs of various kinds (*Figure 74*). The spoon is used for gathering nectar and for other mechanical purposes.

Next time a mosquito bites you capture it but don't crush it, and examine it after first killing it in your insect-killing jar. You will discover that the mandibles, together with the lower jaws, or maxillae, have become modified into piercing organs. They are used to puncture the skin, after which the blood is sucked up. Only the female bites. What, then, does the male do? The male rarely sucks blood, because it is unable to puncture the skin, the mandibles having become aborted and the maxillae only slightly developed. Hence the male has to depend on nectar and the juices of ripe fruits or other sweet substances.

HAVE YOU EVER LOOKED a spider in the eye? Probably not, for few of us ever have the occasion to do so. But let us do it and see what we find.

One of the jumping spiders will do nicely, as they are quite common and easy to find. We need not be afraid to handle spiders, for they are quite harmless, contrary to what most people think. True, they are all poisonous, but the amount of poison they can inject into our skin is so small that we would hardly notice it unless, of course, we are allergic to spider venom. However, it might be best, after capturing a spider, to put it in the killing jar before examining it. There is one spider, the black widow, which has spread over most of our country and can inject enough venom to prove dangerous and in some cases to produce fatal results. So beware of any coal-black spider that is marked with red or yellow or both.

To return to our jumping spiders. They are common on plants, logs, fences, and the sides of buildings, and we need only to step outdoors to find them. They are small or of medium size, measuring about a fourth of an inch or less in length, with short, stout legs, and usually of bright color. They readily attract our attention by their quick jumping movements. Watch one of them for a few moments and you will find that it can move sidewise or backward with great ease. You will also observe that these spiders spin a dragline with which they regain their original position after having leaped in pursuit of some passing insect.

Having watched the antics of the jumping spiders for a while, we now capture one and place it in our killing jar, and when all life has ceased we look at its face with our hand lens. You will be surprised to find that instead of having two eyes the spider seems to have more than that number. Actually the spider has eight eyes, although you may have to look closely to find them all (*Figure 75*). The presence of eight eyes in the jumping spider is not an abnormal phenomenon, as you may think. It is, on the contrary, the normal number in spiders, although in some species two, four, or even six may be lacking.

As we study the eyes carefully we also observe that they vary in size and in arrangement on the head (*Figure 75*). The number and arrangement of the eyes and also, in some instances, the relative size are characteristics much used in classifying spiders. In other words, if you found a spider and wanted to identify it, you would examine the eyes and note the above characteristics, which would serve to indicate the group to which it belonged. From that point it would be relatively easy to complete your identification.

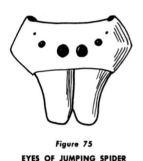

Figure 75
EYES OF JUMPING SPIDER

A spider's eyes have been given different names, according to their position. The normal position of the eyes is in two transverse rows each containing four eyes. The two intermediate eyes of the first row are called the anterior median; the two intermediate eyes of the second row are called posterior median; and the one at each side of the first row anterior lateral and the one at each end of the second row posterior lateral (*Figure 76*).

In the jumping spiders we have a departure from the normal arrangement and also a marked difference in the relative size of the different pairs, characters that enable us to recognize this group at a glance. Instead of two rows there are three. The first row is somewhat curved and consists of four eyes: the anterior median, which are very large, and the two anterior lateral, which are smaller. Behind this first row is a second row, of two eyes: the posterior median, which are very small, and you may have to look very closely to locate them. Behind these two small eyes is still a third row, of two eyes: the posterior lateral.

One more word about the eyes of spiders. Two types of eyes are usually recognized: the so-called nocturnal eyes and the diurnal eyes. Spiders that live in the dark or frequent shady places have eyes that are pearly white in color—they are nocturnal eyes. Diurnal

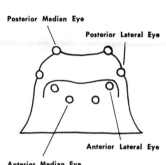

Posterior Median Eye

Posterior Lateral Eye

Anterior Lateral Eye

Anterior Median Eye

Figure 76
EYES OF A SPIDER

eyes, which are typical of most spiders, lack this pearly luster and are variously colored.

One of the most common of our spiders and one we can find at any time of the year is the domestic spider. This is the spider that spins the somewhat unsightly webs we find in a neglected room. It is an exceedingly variable species in color and markings, and if you were to collect a number of them you might well believe that they represent several species. Examine the eyes of this spider and you will find that they are arranged in the normal position of two rows, the anterior row being straight or nearly so (*Figure 77*). Also observe that the two middle pairs of eyes are of the same size and separated from one another and that the lateral eyes of each side are contiguous, that is, adjoining or in contact with one another.

In the early spring, before the grass has grown tall, we often find rather large active spiders running over the ground, sometimes carrying the egg sac attached to them. They are the wolf spiders, hunting spiders which chase their prey. They live on or near the ground and often lurk under stones, especially in damp places. Many species dig tunnels in the earth, and some of them build a turret about the mouth of the tunnel. The famous tarantula of Southern Europe, whose bite was once supposed to cause the dancing

Figure 77
EYES OF DOMESTIC SPIDER

madness, belongs to this group.

The eyes of these wolf spiders are arranged in three rows, as in the jumping spiders, but the relative proportions are very different from what we found in the jumping spiders. The first row consists of four small eyes (*Figure 78*), and the two posterior rows each of two large eyes, the posterior lateral eyes being situated far behind the posterior median eyes.

In the crab spiders we find that the eyes are quite unlike those of the spiders we have examined, not only in size but also in their arrangement. The eyes are all small, dark in color, and arranged in two curved rows. The crab spiders are well named. They have a short and broad body similar to that of the crab and hold their legs in a crablike attitude. Furthermore, they seem to be able to walk more easily sidewise or backward than forward. They are common and rather abundant. Some of them are able to run swiftly and chase their prey; others prefer to lie in wait and pounce on an unsuspecting victim as it passes by. We find them living chiefly on plants and fences and most of them are marked with gray and brown, but a few of them, which conceal themselves in flowers, are brightly colored for purposes of camouflage. One species of crab spider is remarkable for the change in color it undergoes as it

Figure 78
EYES OF A WOLF SPIDER

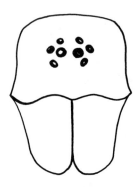

Figure 79
EYES OF GRASS SPIDER

migrates from one colored flower to another. In the spring and early summer it is usually found in white flowers when it is white, thus not only escaping detection by visiting insects but also capturing them without much trouble; later in the season it migrates to yellow flowers, such as goldenrod, and then turns yellow, being then so effectively concealed that it becomes very difficult to locate among the blossoms.

As the summer begins to wane, large, beautiful webs, often as much as two feet in diameter, begin to appear on the grass in meadows and pastures or on other herbaceous growth in marshy places, sometimes even on the shrubs in a garden. You have doubtless seen these webs and perhaps marveled at their construction. You are also probably acquainted with the spider that builds these webs, for it is a fairly large spider and beautifully marked with bands and spots of bright orange. The next time you see one—we know it as the orange garden spider—look at its face with your lens and note that the eyes are all alike, the second row being strongly curved.

Variation seems to be the keynote in the nature world, for differences, though minor, seem to be everywhere, and as we continue to examine the eyes of various spiders we find all sorts of arrangements, though basically they are much the same. In the grass spider, for instance, the two rows of eyes are so strongly curved backward that the anterior median and the posterior lateral eyes form nearly a straight line (*Figure 79*). Speaking of variation, there is a wide range in the size of this spider as well as in the general color. There is also considerable variation in certain structures. All of this makes for considerable confusion, not alone for the amateur student of spiders, but also for the specialist. The grass spider is well named, because its webs are commonly found on grass. Indeed, we seldom realize the immense numbers of webs spun upon the grass by this spider, except when, in early morning, they are made visible by the dew that has condensed upon them. At such times the grass appears to be covered with an almost continuous carpet of silk.

THE GRASSES are a basic form of plant life, performing a dual function as soil binders and as a source of food for many different kinds of animals, including man, since corn, wheat, rye, oats, sugar, and rice are species of grass. In some parts of the world grasses also provide shelter and clothing in the form of bamboo. From earliest spring until late

ADVENTURE 20

We Investigate the Structure of Grass Flowers

Figure 80
SPIKE

Figure 81
PANICLE

autumn the grasses bloom along the wayside and woodland trail, in gardens and orchards, along the banks of winding streams and in waste places, fields, and meadows. Examine the tiny blossoms with your hand lens and you will discover an infinite variety of form and color, and if they are not so garishly or brilliantly colored as the showier flowers more familiar to us, I think you will agree that they are just as beautiful in their rose and lavender, purple and green tints.

As you know, a typical flower consists essentially of sepals and petals, stamens and pistils. When you first look at a grass flower it will appear to bear little resemblance to a lily, which is a typical flower, and if you were to compare the two they would seem to have little in common, that is, structurally. Yet, if the lily you selected for comparison bloomed in a spike and you were to visualize such a lily crowding its flowers, and you were further to reduce the petals to mere scales, the lily would have a reasonably grasslike appearance.

The flowers of grasses are borne in clusters called spikelets, which vary in size and number and which, in turn, are arranged on the main stem in the form of a spike (*Figure 80*) or panicle (*Figure 81*). In a spike the lower spikelets bloom first or from below upward, but in a panicle the uppermost spikelets are

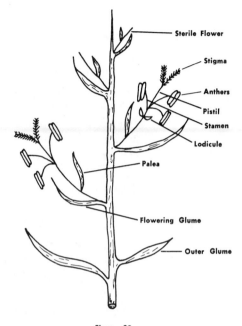

Figure 82

DIAGRAM OF A GRASS FLOWER

the first to blossom, followed successively by those beneath.

When we examine a grass flower carefully with our lens, we find that the sepals and petals have given way to modified leaves called bracts. (And bear in mind that sepals and petals are also modified leaves.) These bracts are called scales or glumes (*Figure 82*) and surround each flower (which the sepals and petals also do in the more conventional flower). The glumes, which are called flowering glumes since there are other kinds, exhibit many interesting peculiarities, often bearing a bristle-like appendage called an awn (*Figure 83*). Awns may be straight, bent, or twisted and either terminate the glumes, when they are known as terminal awns (*Figure 83*), or are borne on the backs of the glumes, when they are said to be dorsal (*Figure 83*). A flowering glume is keeled when it is flattened and folded so that its two edges are brought closely together and the midvein is prominent as a ridge on the back of the scale. When the veins of the glumes are conspicuous, the glume is considered to be three-nerved, five-nerved, seven-nerved, or nine-nerved, according to the number of prominent veins (*Figure 84*).

We had to digress for a moment in order to provide a description of the flowering scales, but now, to return to the flower, we observe that opposite the flowering glume is an awnless glume called the palea (*Figure 82*). It is usually thin in texture and two-nerved, showing two green keels. At the base of the flower are usually two (rarely three) minute, thin, and translucent glumes called lodicules (*Figure 82*). The lodicules are rarely noticed except at the time of flowering, when for a short time they become swollen with sap and, by pressing the flowering glume and

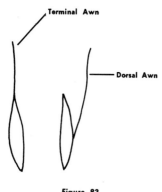

Terminal Awn

Dorsal Awn

Figure 83
AWNED GLUMES

palea apart, cause the blossom to open.

As we examine various grass flowers, we find that most of them are perfect, that is, bear both stamens and pistils (*Figure 82*). There are one to six (usually three) stamens whose very slender filaments bear two-celled anthers. The anthers are lightly attached near the middle to the apex of the filament and when they tremble in the wind easily discharge the pollen grains. Since the grasses must depend upon the wind for pollination, a vast number of pollen grains are produced to ensure sufficient seed. It has been estimated that a single anther of rye contains no less than twenty thousand pollen grains. You will find that most grasses of spring have larger anthers than those of midsummer, but brilliant colors, ranging from yellow to orange and crimson, and from lavender to deep purple, appear in the anthers throughout the entire flowering season. The feathery stigmas frequently show a conspicuous color too.

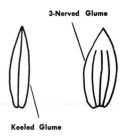

3-Nerved Glume

Keeled Glume

Figure 84
KEELED GLUMES

YOU WILL RECALL that in the discussion of the aphids (Adventure 17) I said that these insects could become a scourge if it were not for their enemies. One of the most effective in keeping them in check is the aphis lion.

ADVENTURE 21

We Hunt a Lion

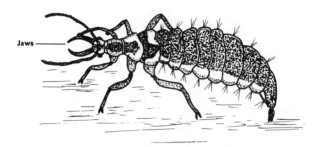

Jaws

Figure 85
APHIS LION

The aphis lion is not a particularly pre-possessing-looking creature, as you will see when you look at one through your lens, with its spindle-shaped body and its peculiarly long, sickle-shaped jaws, which project from its head (*Figure 85*). These jaws are effectual instruments for grasping the soft-bodied aphids and, since they are hollow, with an opening at each end, the opening at the base leading into the lion's throat, they also serve as efficient suction tubes.

Though the aphis lion bears no resemblance to the four-footed mammal of the jungle, it is well named if we think of it in predatory terms. It is a bloodthirsty creature, preying almost exclusively on aphids and sucking their blood until nothing is left of a victim but a shriveled-up mass of skin. Com-

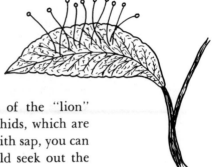

Figure 86
EGGS OF APHIS LION

paring the evil-looking jaws of the "lion" with the soft bodies of the aphids, which are usually extended or swollen with sap, you can readily see why the lion would seek out the aphids, since they provide it with an easily available food supply. Usually the lions are not hard pressed to locate the aphids, since the mother aphis lion generally lays her eggs in a colony of aphids so that her young, when they hatch, have food ready at hand.

After you have watched an aphis lion feed on the aphids, look for the eggs. They are easily seen for each egg is placed on the tip of a slender stalk (*Figure 86*). Examine the eggs carefully and you should be able to detect the little doubled-up and still-unhatched lions. You may even find one about to emerge from its egg. Watch closely and you will see the jaws thrust through the shell, opening it, as it were, for a peephole. Then the head gradually appears, followed by the legs and finally by the spindle-shaped body. Now what does this newly emerged lion do? It appears in no hurry to descend the stalk, but clings to the eggshell while it looks about at its new surroundings. Eventually, as if it were satisfied with what it sees, it begins to climb about the eggshell until it discovers the stalk. Since there is now no place to go but down the stalk, it grasps the stalk with its first pair of legs and with the help of the other two pairs of legs begins a careful descent, a feat for a creature only a few minutes old and with no previous experience at such gymnastics. At last it arrives safely on the surface of the leaf and pauses for a moment to look around. Spying the nearby aphids and without further ado, it proceeds to satisfy its hunger.

You may ask why the eggs were placed separately on the tips of stalks instead of being laid in a mass on the surface of the leaf. The explanation is a simple one and at the same time illustrates an interesting provision of nature. The carnivorous lions that hatch from the eggs would just as soon eat one another or the unhatched eggs as search for aphids. But as the eggs hatch one at a time and since there is nothing to eat but an inedible stalk, the newly hatched "lion" must perforce descend the stalk in order to find something to eat. Of course, it could ascend the neighboring stalks and feed on its unhatched brothers and sisters, but how much better merely to seize the helpless and defenseless aphids that are at hand for the taking.

The mother aphis lion appears so entirely

unlike her offspring that it would be difficult to believe they are related. Have you ever observed a small green insect with golden eyes and delicate, lacelike wings flying about? That is the mother, commonly known as the ˙ˌˌˌg ʋut sometimes as the golden-eyed lacewing.

If you can find a mother lacewing in the act of laying her eggs, watch how she does it. You will need your lens, of course, or, better still, your reading glass. You will observe that first she deposits a drop of sticky fluid that she ejects from the tip of her body on the surface of the leaf. Then she lifts up her slender abdomen and spins the drop into a thread, a half inch long or more, that hardens almost immediately upon exposure to the air. She next lays an oblong egg about the size of a pin point on the tip of the thread or stalk and, with this accomplished, proceeds to spin another stalk and lay another egg. She repeats this performance until she has laid her full complement of eggs.

THE STUDY OF NATURE or the outdoors is the study of life itself. No one has yet been able to define life to anyone's complete satisfaction, and, of course, no one has been able to create life, although we seem to be on the

ADVENTURE 22

*We Trace
a Tadpole's
Development*

verge of doing so. How a complex organism can develop from a microscopic egg, after it has been induced to grow through union with a microscopic sperm, is still one of the greatest mysteries, even though we know a great deal of what takes place.

Let us watch a tadpole develop from an egg. As this is a seasonal occurrence, we must be prepared to collect the eggs as soon as they are laid. Frog eggs are usually laid in April, but the exact time depends on the locality and the weather. About the first of the month prepare an aquarium or battery jar to receive the eggs. The aquarium or jar should have several inches of clean soil and of water and be planted with several washed aquatic plants to provide aeration. Then select a pond or spring pool—one near your home if possible—where you know frogs congregate each spring to mate, and visit it every day, taking along a bucket or pail, until you find the eggs. They are laid in rounded, gelatinous masses in shallow water and may be attached to sticks and grasses or left free in the water. In the masses the eggs look like small beads, each surrounded by a transparent covering. The jelly protects the eggs from injury and makes it more difficult for fish to eat them. Transfer the eggs to the bucket with your cupped hand, or take along a small pan or dipper for the purpose. Be careful not to pour the eggs or disturb them unnecessarily. As the eggs begin to develop within two or three hours after they have been laid, it is important, if you want to watch the development of the tadpole from the very beginning, to collect the eggs as soon as possible after they are laid.

On arriving home with the eggs allow them to remain in the bucket until the temperature of the water is the same as that of the water in the previously filled aquarium or jar. When the temperatures are the same, transfer the eggs to the aquarium or jar, using the same care as when you collected them. A mass of frog eggs the size of your hand requires about five gallons of water for proper aeration, so if you have a smaller or larger aquarium use only a proportionate size of the egg mass.

Now examine an egg with your lens. You will find it extremely small (about one and a half millimeters in diameter), surrounded by its perfectly transparent sphere of jelly. Note that about two thirds of it is velvety black in color, the remainder, or lower side, creamy white. The black area is the future tadpole and the white area is the food yolk for growth (*Figure 87*).

The first sign of beginning development is a slight increase in size. At the same time the black area spreads until the visible white

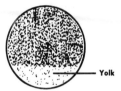

Figure 87
EGG OF FROG

portion becomes no larger than a pin point. Then a groove appears in the mid-line at the top of the egg. This groove increases in length until it completely encircles the egg, and provides external evidence that the egg has divided into two equal parts (*Figure 88A*). Next a second groove appears at right angles to the first and rapidly encircles the egg until it has become divided into four nearly equal parts (*Figure 88B*). A further subdivision is made by a horizontal partition instead of a vertical one. This partition and its external groove are somewhat above the center of the egg so that the upper portion is smaller than the lower (*Figure 88C*). From this time on further subdivisions are more rapid and more irregular and it becomes increasingly difficult to follow them since they become too small to be readily seen. What you have actually seen so far is the egg, which is a single cell, first dividing into two cells, then the two cells dividing into four, and so on until there is eventually formed a ball-like mass of many, many cells. Biologists call this mass of cells a blastula, but we shall continue to refer to it as the egg.

If you look carefully at an egg on the second day (after they are laid), you should see a dark crescent-shaped line on one side just below the middle (*Figure 88D*). Twelve hours later you will find that this crescent has be-

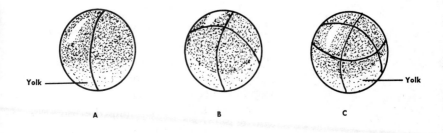

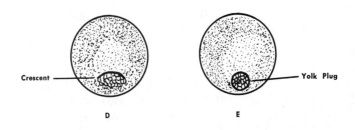

Figure 88
DEVELOPMENT OF FROG'S EGG

come a circle (*Figure 88E*). You will now also observe that the black surface of the egg has spread almost to the edges of the circle and that the circle itself encloses a mass of white yolk that protrudes like a small cushion. This circle, with its protruding plug of yolk, is the external indication that the cells have begun to separate and are beginning to form the digestive tract. As this tract begins forming at the posterior instead of the head end, the yolk plug marks a point very near the posterior end of the tadpole, or young frog.

On the third day you will find that the eggs have become elongated and that a groove is forming lengthwise along the top (*Figure 89*). Since this groove marks the back of the developing tadpole, it is easy to see which is to be the head and which is to be the tail and which are to be the right and left sides.

By the fourth day the eggs have greatly changed. They have become more elongated and the yolk plug has retreated. The groove, which began so simply, has now become extended along the entire length of the back (top of egg) and two folds of the surface are slowly rolling in over it, one on each side. Both the groove and the folds will form a tube that is the beginning of the nervous system, the head end forming the brain and the remainder the spinal cord.

You will observe that on the next day the eggs have become even more elongated and also that the head and tail ends have curved somewhat to one side. Note, too, that the line of the back is nearly straight and that the yolk side is very convex. The nerve tube now appears to be entirely closed in, but the folds persist over the head and along the back. The projection that is to form the tail is quite noticeable.

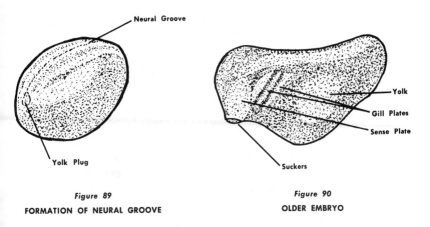

Figure 89
FORMATION OF NEURAL GROOVE

Figure 90
OLDER EMBRYO

Look at the egg, or the developing embryo, either from above or from below, and you should see slight projections or swellings in the region of the head and neck (*Figure 90*). The largest swelling (sense plate) will become the facial part of the head, with upper and lower jaws, mouth, and nostrils. The three smaller swellings will become the gills. There is also a blunt projection or swelling on the lower part of the head end. Viewed from the front, it becomes one side of a horseshoe-shaped structure and will eventually develop into a pair of suckers that will be used by the tadpole to attach itself to waterweeds.

By the end of the sixth day the young developing tadpoles have become even longer and more curved. The body is thinner, the head and tail ends are unmistakable, and the swellings on the sides of the neck more distinct. On the following day the head is more delineated and the tail is longer and clearly finned at its edges. You may observe the tadpoles move occasionally.

Nine days after the eggs are laid the tadpoles are out of the jelly, clinging, by means of their suckers, to the deserted jelly mass or water plants. The suckers do not act in the way their names would seem to imply but function by reason of a sticky substance or cement they secrete. If all the tadpoles are not out of the jelly, you should be able to see some of them hatch from the egg: with a vigorous wriggle a tadpole escapes from the egg, the jelly ruptures, and the tadpole is free. Note that the tadpoles are very slender and black and that the transparent tail is quite conspicuous. Observe, too, that the swellings at the sides of the neck are branched, fingerlike gills. With your lens examine the tadpole closely and you will see the swellings that are to become eyes, and an opening just forward of the suckers that is to be the mouth.

On the following day all the tadpoles should be out of their eggs. They hang quietly from the water plants or circle about with vigorous wrigglings of the tail whenever disturbed. Through the next few days further changes take place. The tadpoles become longer, although the increase in length is mainly in the tail, and they also become wider, due to the further development of internal organs. Then, on the sixteenth day, they are swimming about rapidly, with mouths open, and nibbling at the water plants. They are no longer jet black but rather brownish, with a fine mottling of gold spots on the back.

MANY OF THE WAYS in which nature has contrived to effect seed dispersal are most ingenious. The seeds of some plants, as those of the dandelion, are provided with silken hairs that catch in the wind; others are able to float on water and in that manner are transported to distant places. Then there are those plants that shoot or propel their seeds considerable distances into the air, as the witch hazel. Finally, we have the plants whose seeds are furnished with structures that catch in the fur of animals or in our clothing when we come in contact with them.

Most familiar of these so-called "hitch-hikers" are the burs that occur on a familiar and rather rank-odored weed called the burdock, which is common along roadsides and

ADVENTURE 23

We Encounter Some Hitchhikers

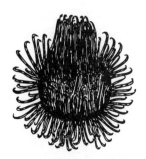

Figure 91
BURDOCK

Figure 91A
AKENE OF BURDOCK

in waste places. The leaves are large, dull green, and woolly on the lower surface, and the flowers, which blossom in globular flower heads, are small, light magenta, and often nearly white. When the flowers have "gone to seed" or, more accurately, have developed into fruits, the entire flower head has become the bur shown in *Figure 91*. If we look at it through our lens, we can readily see why it clings so tenaciously to our clothing. It consists of a number of individual fruits called akenes (sometimes spelled achenes), and if you examine one of these akenes closely you will find it appears as in *Figure 91A*. It is somewhat oblong in shape, three-angled, ribbed, and truncate, that is, one end appears as if cut off transversely. The other end is fashioned in the form of a hook. Need we say more?

Even more exasperating when it comes to removing them from our clothing are the beggar-ticks. The beggar-ticks are also akenes and are formed on a number of related plants, as the bur marigold, tickseed sunflower, Spanish needles, and the beggar-ticks, also known as the sticktight. These plants form a group of rather uninteresting weeds with various leaves and mostly yellow flowers. The akenes are much alike except that they may vary somewhat in shape, being wedge-shaped, linear, or oblong. The akene shown in *Figure 92* is from the beggar-ticks, which can usually be found growing in damp situations. Sometimes my trousers have been so completely covered with these akenes that it has taken me hours to get them off. Look at one with your lens and see why. *Figure 93* shows an akene from Spanish needles. It resembles the akene of beggar-ticks except that it is four-awned, whereas the former is two-awned.

If we should walk in the woods during July or August, we would likely come upon a plant having a generally leafless flower stem with a scattered cluster of very small magenta-pink or lilac flowers and known as the tick trefoil. A few weeks later, were we to return to this same plant, we would find that the flowers had developed into seed pods shaped somewhat like that in *Figure 94*. To our naked eye there would be no apparent reason why these seed pods should become attached to our clothing, as they do should we brush against them. But we need only to view them through our lens to see that they are provided with minute hooked hairs that are as effective in hitchhiking a ride as the barbed akenes of the beggar-ticks or the hooked akenes of the burdock. There are many species of tick trefoils, each with its own characteristically shaped seed pods, so that if you find pods slightly different in shape from that illus-

Figure 92
BEGGAR-TICKS

Figure 93
SPANISH NEEDLES

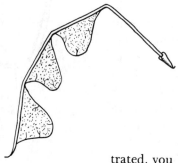

Figure 94
TICK TREFOIL

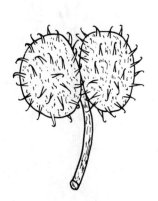

Figure 95
CLEAVERS

trated, you know the reason why.

Frequently a plant has some characteristic structure that has invited a variety of names descriptive of that particular structure. Such a plant is the one commonly called cleavers or goose grass. Other names, such as catch-weed, burhead, cling-rascal, scratch grass, wild hedgeburs, stick-a-back, and grip or gripgrass, are more appropriate. Perhaps most of these names have been given to it because the stems are furnished with backward-hooked prickles, but they are also descriptive of the burlike fruits, which occur in pairs and which are covered with short, hooked bristles (*Figure 95*). Look for this plant in shady thickets and along roadsides. You can recognize it by its prickly, reclining stem and by the two tiny white blossoms.

There are many other plants whose fruits have been modified for transportation by animals. One of them is the cocklebur, whose burs are provided with hooked prickles (*Fig-*

ure 96). Look for it in waste places. Another is the wild carrot, or Queen Anne's lace, whose flat-topped clusters of white flowers are conspicuous on the summer landscape. The fruit is oblong in shape, rather flattened, and has four wings armed with bristles. As you look at these and many others in the course of your explorations, you will become increasingly aware of the countless designs that nature has devised for the survival of the many different plant species.

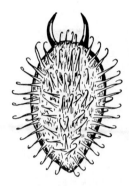

Figure 96
COCKLEBUR

CADDIS WORMS are not worms, but the larval form of the caddis fly, an insect that looks something like a moth except that its body is more slender and it is more delicately built.

Caddis worms are of considerable interest because they build houses or cases that they carry around much in the manner of the snails. But whereas all kinds of snails build houses of the same kind of material, the caddis worms use different materials. Some build of sticks, which they fasten together lengthwise, and some put the sticks together crosswise, like log cabins. Others construct their houses out of a hollow stem or of bits of leaves (*Figure 97*), and still others make use of sand (*Figure 98*) and pebbles (*Figure 99*). Then there are those that make use of rubbish and

ADVENTURE 24

We Make the Acquaintance of Some Housebuilders

Figure 97
CASE MADE FROM BITS OF LEAVES

Figure 98
CASE MADE OF SAND GRAINS

silk and fashion these materials together in the form of a little cornucopia. All of them, however, use their own saliva to cement the materials together. Since each species builds its own distinctive dwelling, each kind of house is thus a clue to the identity of its occupant.

Caddis worms may be found in almost any brook or pond throughout the summer, and a few can be found even in winter. They can be seen with the naked eye seemingly as pebbles or sticks or dead leaves moving in the water. Only by means of our lens, however, can we learn how the houses are put together or study the occupants. We can easily remove them from the water by picking them up with our fingers or by using a pan or scoop.

As you examine the dwelling you will see that it is open at both ends, with a front and back door, as it were. The caddis worm may not be visible at first, for as you remove it from the water it becomes frightened and retires into the house. If you do not disturb it, its dark-colored head will soon appear and then emerge, followed by the six pairs of legs. This is how it appears as it moves about the bottom of the brook or pond.

Now take hold of it and by pulling gently remove it from its house. First of all note that it is wormlike in form (*Figure 100*). Next observe the little tassels of short, threadlike white gills along the sides of the abdomen. Water is made to pass over these gills by undulating movements of the body. The water enters through one opening of the house, flows over the gills, and then out through the other opening, hence the reason for front and back doors. See if you can locate three tubercles (*Figure 100*). They serve to keep the body from pressing against the edge of the opening and thus preventing the water from entering.

The caddis worm manages to hold on to its house, as it crawls about, by a pair of curved hooks (*Figure 100*) that are called grabhooks.

Unlike the snail, which is attached to its house, the caddis worm is not grown fast to its case. You can discover this by holding the case down on a flat surface with its occupant wrong side up, using your finger or a pair of forceps for the purpose. After a few struggles the caddis worm will succeed in turning itself over within its case.

Although you may not be able to observe to the smallest detail how a caddis worm builds its house, you can watch the general procedure. Get a caddis worm that is about half grown, remove a section of the front part of its house, and then place the insect in a tumbler with a little water in it and containing a few bits of brightly colored flower petals. Within a few hours the little house

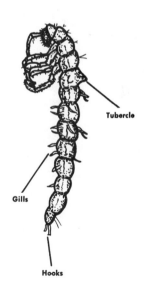

Tubercle

Gills

Hooks

Figure 100
CADDIS FLY LARVA

will look like a blossom, with several rows of petals rimming the opening.

ADVENTURE 25

We Come Upon Some More Housebuilders

IN OUR LAST ADVENTURE we discussed the portable dwellings of the caddis worms. These insects are not the only ones that build temporary shelters, although they are probably the most advanced in this form of insect behavior. Actually most orders are represented by species that illustrate the habit.

These shelters, or houses, or dwellings, as we have variously called them, are known more accurately as cases, and the insects that construct them as case-makers or case-bearers. As we shall see, not all cases are portable; some are permanently or semi-permanently attached, and even the portable ones are never completely portable, for they become attached to some object when the larvae are ready to pupate. This is equally true of the caddis worms.

As the case-making insects represent almost all the orders, we would expect that the cases they construct would vary in form and materials used as much as the insects themselves exhibit different types of behavioral patterns. Thus we have cases that are very simple affairs, while others are more complex. Some are merely a sheet of silk or a silken tube; others consist of various materials added or blended with the silk, but all have in common the use of silk as the primary material.

Much can be written about the origin and development of the case-making habit, but what we are particularly interested in at present is to find and examine a few typical cases and to observe how they are put together. Since many of them serve as winter retreats for the hibernating larvae, we can engage in this study almost any time of the year. However, if we wish to observe the habits of the larvae, we can do so only when they are active and feeding, during the warmer months. An exception would be the clothes moths, which may be found throughout the year. It may be somewhat difficult to find these insects, for no one will admit their presence, since to do so would be a confession of neglect. Yet you may come across them sometimes. Should you do so, transfer a few of the cases with their occupants to a bottle or jar. You can then observe with your lens how the larvae have to enlarge their cases from time to time to accommodate an increase in size The cases are simply silken tubes in which bits of material on which the insects feed are sometimes incorporated (*Figure 101*).

Far more available are the curious baglike shelters of the bagworm (*Figure 102*). This

Figure 101
SILKEN CASE OF CLOTHES MOTH

Figure 102
CASE OF BAGWORM

Figure 103
CASE OF CIGAR CASEMAKER

insect feeds on a variety of shade trees, shrubs, and hedges, but has a particular fondness for the arborvitae and red cedar, so look for the "bags" on these trees. The best time is during July and August, when the larvae are growing and feeding; they may also be found in the winter. As the cases measure from three quarters of an inch to one and a half inches long they are not difficult to find. Note that they are made of bits of bark or pieces of foliage bound together into a silk-lined case.

In some instances the cases resemble well-known objects. One such case is shaped in the form of a cigar (*Figure 103*), hence its maker is known as the cigar case-maker or case-bearer. It measures about five sixteenths of an inch in length and is brown in color. Being so small, it may take a little searching. A reading glass should help you to locate it. While you are searching for it, you may also keep your eyes open for a black case shaped like a pistol (*Figure 104*). Both the cigar case-bearer and the pistol case-bearer are pests of the apple and feed on the leaves to which they eventually attach their cases. The insects appear when the leaves begin to unfold, so the best time of the year to find them is in early spring or during the period of their larval development, from April to July.

Frequently a small oval case about five eighths of an inch long may be found on a

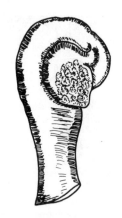

Figure 104
CASE OF PISTOL CASEMAKER

leaf of the sugar maple (*Figure 105*). The maker of the case, called the maple-leaf cutter, is a rather interesting little insect. The larva cuts an oval-shaped piece of leaf and attaches it to the leaf by means of silk. At first it lives between the leaf and the piece fastened down, but later it cuts around the oval piece of leaf and fastens the two together to form a new case, which, in turn, it attaches to the surface of the leaf. When it needs new feeding grounds it merely cuts the supporting strands and wanders off with its case.

These cases are only a few of the many you can find by exploring your neighborhood. The best time, of course, is during the summer, but, surprisingly, a few, as those of the resplendent shield-bearer (*Figure 106*), can be found on the twigs and trunks of various trees and shrubs during the winter. They are well worth the effort spent in looking for them, since they provide an interesting facet to the study of insect behavior, one of the most absorbing fields for investigation.

Figure 105
CASE OF MAPLE-LEAF CUTTER

Figure 106
CASES OF RESPLENDENT SHIELD-BEARER

LEECHES ARE COMMON in our ponds and streams, and most of us know them. Some of us have even had the unfortunate experience of having been bitten by them. Their bites are not dangerous except through an inci-

ADVENTURE 26

We Ascertain how the Leech Sucks Blood

dental infection of the wound, but they can cause an intense itching if they are removed before they are allowed to finish their meal.

Leeches are generally marked with concealing colors and patterns—browns, greens, and blacks—which serve to render them inconspicuous among the broken shadows and water-soaked leaves of their environment. Though some species feed on worms and snails, and a few are scavengers or even cannibals, most of them suck blood. Sometimes they attack animals, as frogs and turtles, in such numbers that they literally drain them of their lifeblood.

Leeches do not have to swim about in search of a meal. They are acutely sensitive to the slightest vibration of the water, to shadows passing over them, and to the smallest amount of any substance dissolved in the water around them. You can observe this for yourself by merely placing a few of them in a dish and then pressing your finger against the bottom of it. They will immediately begin to crawl about and restlessly explore the entire surface of the dish. Should they pass over your fingerprint, they would become quite agitated in response to its odor. Any movement in the water of a pond also makes them very excited. That is why, should you wade into a pond where leeches are abundant, they will become attached to your legs within a matter of minutes. Incidentally, this is a good way to collect them, but I would suggest that you wear rubber boots, since the leeches do not wholly rely on the odor of flesh and will just as readily become attached to boots.

Leeches have the means to fasten themselves to almost any kind of surface. Examine one and you will find a strong muscular sucker at each end, the posterior one being larger (*Figure 107*). Look at the posterior sucker through your lens and you will readily see why it functions as well as it does. You are familiar with the "plumber's helper," which consists merely of a rubber cup attached to the end of a wooden stick, or the small rubber suction cups that are used to display merchandise on a store window. Both of these devices and the leech's sucker operate in the same manner: by excluding air from within the cup the unequal air pressures thus created within the cup and on its exterior surface keep the suction cup in place.

When a bloodsucking leech (and bear in mind that I said not all leeches are bloodsuckers) finds a likely skin surface, it attaches its posterior sucker and then swings its head about in a manner of exploration. It prefers a spot where the skin is broken or is well supplied with blood vessels. Upon locating a satisfactory spot it presses down its anterior

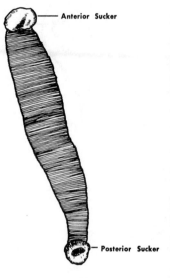

Anterior Sucker

Posterior Sucker

Figure 107
VENTRAL VIEW OF LEECH
SHOWING SUCKERS

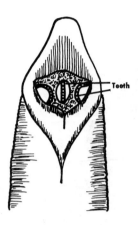

sucker and then makes a wound in the flesh with its three jaws. Look at the anterior sucker and you will note the small, oval mouth. With your lens you should also be able to see the jaws and teeth (*Figure 108*). For sucking the blood the animal is provided with a sort of suction bulb in the pharynx, or throat cavity, which can be seen only upon dissection.

The salivary gland of the leech secretes a substance called hirudin, which prevents the blood from coagulating and keeps it thin so that it can easily be sucked up. When the jaws break the skin, this hirudin pours into the wound, which at first is painless, though it may itch intensely later on. If, however, the leech is permitted to finish its meal, there should be no itching. The reason is that the hirudin, which causes the itching, has by then been completely sucked up with the blood.

A leech doesn't have to eat very often, because as it feeds the fluid part of the blood is drawn off through the kidneys and the solid matter stored in lateral pouches of the digestive tract as a sort of reserve food supply. Leeches have been kept in aquariums for as long as fifteen months with only a single feeding. So, if you are interesting in studying these animals, you can do so with a minimum of care. All you need is a bottle partially filled with water, and a piece of mosquito netting or similar material tied over the mouth to prevent the animals from crawling out. A meal of ground meat, beef liver, or earthworms will do them for several weeks. Be sure to change the water each day to provide them with a fresh supply of oxygen and to prevent the water from becoming polluted. In observing their habits I would suggest a reading glass, although for close observation a hand lens should be used. In olden times leeches were used in bloodletting, and I read lately that the practice is being revived; some drugstores again carry them.

ADVENTURE 27

We Identify Some Ferns

FERNS ARE NOT a particularly important form of plant life. However, it was not always so. At one time they and their allies were the dominant plants of the earth. They are generally supposed to be the oldest form of terrestrial vegetation now in existence, and the coal we now mine is said to have been formed from their remains many millions of years ago. At that time they grew to an enormous size, often attaining a height of fifty feet or more. Some of the ferns found in the tropical rain forests today grow to considerable heights, but the ferns with which most of us are familiar are low-growing species.

There are many kinds of ferns, and though,

at a glance, they may appear to be much alike, they all differ from one another if only slightly. Sometimes only an expert can recognize certain species. Many of them can readily be recognized by their habits of growth, by the shapes of their fronds, or by the manner in which the fronds have been cut, so we need not be an expert to know at least a few of them. Once we have become familiar with such easily recognizable species as the bracken, the sensitive fern, and the common polypody, for example, we can go a little further and learn how to identify others by their fruit dots. These fruit dots appear as little brown or gray specks or dots on the lower surface of the frond; perhaps you have noticed them.

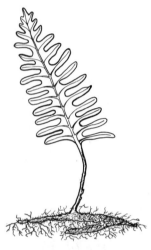

Before we continue, let me point out that a frond is merely a leaf. In most ferns the fronds have been cut into divisions or leaflets called pinnae, and in some species these divisions have been further subdivided into still smaller leaflets, or pinnules. Ferns reproduce by means of spores, which are produced in small structures called sporangia (singular sporangium). These sporangia are usually clustered in groups called sori (singular sorus), which occur in various shapes in the different species. Thus they may be linear, oblong, kidney-shaped, or curved. Their shape and position on the frond, or more accurately on the pinnae, serve as a means of identification.

Let us consider the common polypody (*Figure 108A*). This fern is one of the most abundant and ubiquitous of our fern species and may easily be recognized by its evergreen fronds, which are deeply divided into long, narrow, usually obtuse segments that almost reach the midrib, and by its general habit of growing among shaded rocks in the woods. Since the fruit dots are visible to the naked eye, we need only glance at the lower surface of the fronds to find whether they are there. Fruit dots are not always present on the ferns; since they are reproductive structures, they occur only at certain times. Should we look at the polypody frond at the right time of the year and examine the fruit dots with our lens, we would find them rather large, yellow-brown in color, roundish in form, and located midway between the mid-vein and margin of the pinnae (*Figure 109*). These features, namely color, form, and position, are peculiar to the polypody and thus serve as diagnostic characters that would enable us to identify this fern if we could not otherwise readily do so by the shape of its frond, habit of growing, or some other outstanding characteristic.

If we should next examine the fruit dots of the silvery spleenwort (*Figure 109A*), a

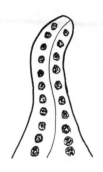

Figure 109
FRUIT DOTS OF COMMON POLYPODY

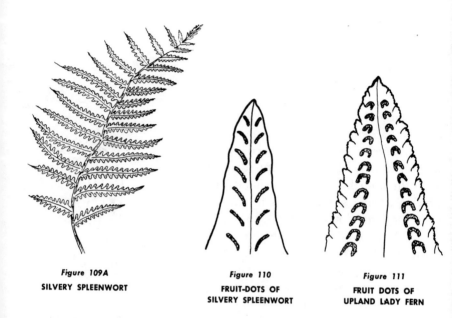

fern with fronds two feet or more long and also found in the woods but usually in wet ground, we would find the fruit dots quite unlike those of the polypody. They are numerous, slightly curving, and oblong and are arranged in a double row at an angle to the midveins of the pinnules (*Figure 110*). So far we have seen how the fruit dots of these two ferns differ. Let us take a third species—the upland lady fern. Here the fruit dots are horseshoe-shaped and curve away from the midveins (*Figure 111*). There appear to be all sorts of variations in the ap-

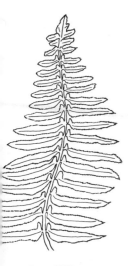

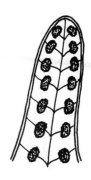

Figure 111A
CHRISTMAS FERN

Figure 112
FRUIT DOTS OF CHRISTMAS FERN

Figure 113
FRUIT DOTS OF MARSH FERN

pearance and position of the fruit dots as we
examine one fern after another. Thus, in the
Christmas fern (*Figure 111A*), they are round
and arranged in two lengthwise rows near
the midveins (*Figure 112*), and in the marsh
fern they are small and kidney-shaped in two
rows parallel to and near the midveins (*Figure 113*). There is no denying that the variations found in the fruit dots provide us with
another facet of nature's working, but, what
is perhaps more to the point, furnish us with
an easy and interesting way of becoming acquainted with the ferns.

*We View
the Scale Insects*

Figure 114
PINE-LEAF SCALE

SOMETIMES WE FIND pine needles covered with what appears to be a white powder. If we examined it with our lens, we would discover that it is not a powder but a mass of long and narrow snowy-white scales (*Figure 114*). If these scales further intrigued us and we pried one off with a fingernail and looked at it closely, we would find that it is some sort of an animal, possibly an insect. We would not be mistaken in our conclusion, for what we had observed on the pine needle is known as the pine-leaf scale, one of a large group of insects known as scale insects.

There are many different species and as a group present a number of interesting and curious features. The males do not have a mouth and have only a single pair of wings, although in a few species they are entirely wingless or have only vestigial wings. As with the true flies (See Adventure 10), their hind wings have been replaced by a pair of club-like halteres. Unlike the males, the females are always wingless, and so are the young, and the females in some species are legless, too. The females have either a scale-like or gall-like form or they may be grublike and clothed with wax. The waxy covering may be in the form of powder, large tufts, plates, a continuous layer, or a thin scale beneath which the insect lives.

All scale insects suck plant juices, and

though most of them occur on leaves and stems, a few infest the roots of their host plants. Some species are quite restricted in food habits, while others can feed on a variety of plants. Because they suck the plant juices, they are injurious and can cause considerable damage when they become abundant. Some scale insects, however, are not harmful; a few species, as the lac insect, which supplies us with shellac, are useful. At one time various dyes were obtained from certain species, but these dyes today are made from coal tar. Wax, too, was formerly obtained from these insects; candles were once made in China exclusively from such wax.

One of the commonest and most widely distributed of the scale insects in our country is the oyster-shell scale. It is usually found on fruit trees and various shrubs, but also occurs on other plants. Lilac branches are sometimes covered with it. The scales may be seen with the naked eye, but are better observed with the lens. They are curved like oystershells, are about one eighth of an inch long, and their brownish color matches the dark bark (*Figure 115*). If you examine these scales in winter, you will find upward of a hundred white eggs beneath each scale together with the dead body of the female. The winter is passed in the egg stage, and in the following spring minute yellowish young emerge, in-

Figure 115
OYSTER-SHELL SCALE

Figure 116
SAN JOSE SCALE

Figure 117
ROSE SCALE

sert their sucking tubes in the bark, and begin to feed.

Perhaps the best known of all our scale insects is the San Jose scale. It is also the most notorious because of the enormous losses it inflicted at one time upon fruit trees. It was the cause of considerable legislation leading to the development of comprehensive quarantine in this country. It infects many varieties of fruit trees and garden shrubs, and if you live in a region where the winters do not get too cold, you should have no trouble finding it. The female is yellowish in color, circular in form, without legs, and slightly smaller then the head of a pin. She is covered with a dark gray circular, waxy scale, one sixteenth of an inch in diameter, slightly elevated in the center into a nipple formed by cast-off skins and surrounded by a ring that varies from pale yellow to a reddish yellow (*Figure 116*). Smaller black scales somewhat elongate in form are the males.

Sometimes the stems of rosebushes present a whitish scurfy appearance, evidence of attack by the rose scale. The scales of the female are circular (*Figure 117*), snowy white, and if you were to examine them in winter, you would likely find masses of purplish eggs concealed beneath them. White scales that are irregularly oval, with a yellowish point and about a tenth of an inch long, denote the presence of the scurvy scale, a common pest of the apple but not particularly destructive. I can recall the first time I happened to come across the cottony maple scale. I was doing some collecting along a brookside when my eye was attracted to what appeared to be bits of cotton stuck on several twigs of a maple. Curious to know how they had gotten there, I went closer to investigate and found that they were actually tufts of a cottony material protruding from oval brown scales (*Figure 118*). The cottony maple scale is common on maple, Osage orange, and grape, and during the summer it is not unusual to find the twigs of these plants festooned with the cottony tufts.

Figure 118
COTTONY MAPLE SCALE

THE DICTIONARY DEFINES a mineral as any chemical element or compound occurring naturally as a product of inorganic processes. It says further that it is usually a solid of a definite molecular composition and that it occurs, except in rare instances, in crystal form. The question now arises, what is meant by crystal form? Again referring to the dictionary, we find that crystal form refers to any solid form having plane surfaces symmetrically arranged. Let us go into the kitchen and dissolve some ordinary table salt

ADVENTURE 29

*We Undertake
the Study
of Minerals*

in a little water. When it has completely dissolved, we place a drop of the solution on a piece of glass. We wait until the water has evaporated and then examine the residue with our lens. What do we find? Small, perfectly shaped cubes of salt—in other words, salt crystals (*Figure 119*).

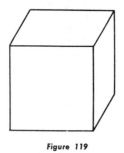

Figure 119
CRYSTAL OF SALT (HALITE)

By chemical analysis salt is shown to consist of one atom of sodium and one atom of chlorine. Since it is therefore of a definite molecular composition, it must be a compound. Thus it satisfies the above definition of a mineral. As a mineral it is known as halite (*Figure 119*).

Let us next examine another very common mineral, water. You might question my calling water a mineral. But it has a definite molecular composition, being formed of two atoms of hydrogen and one atom of oxygen and chemically known as hydrogen oxide; it is a solid (ice); and as a solid it crystallizes. You certainly have heard of snow crystals, which are simply crystals of solid water or ice. You can see them at any time of the year. Scrape some ice from the inside of your refrigerator onto a piece of glass and look at it with your lens. Water crystallizes as hexagonal, or six-sided, pyramids, but since several crystals are usually grouped together they may not be very sharply defined.

A third common mineral generally available is quartz, known chemically as silicon dioxide or silica. Everyone is so familiar with this mineral that it seems hardly necessary to say anything about it. In general appearance it resembles glass except that it is crystalline in form, whereas glass is amorphous, or without form. It occurs in many varieties. Amethyst, carnelian, opal, chalcedony, agate are all color varieties. But the quartz, as we mostly know it, is colorless and transparent. If you can locate a piece of pure quartz, you will observe that its usual form is a hexagonal prism (*Figure 120*). Quartz, however, also occurs in grains or masses. Ordinary sand is composed in part of quartz grains; they are actually the chief constituent of river and beach sands. Obtain some of this sand (the sand sold in stores for cage birds will do) and examine it with your lens. You should recognize the quartz grains easily. They are not crystalline but are rounded or irregularly shaped, due to the action of wind and water.

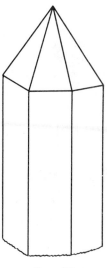

Figure 120
CRYSTAL OF QUARTZ

ALTHOUGH TREES are a familiar and conspicuous feature of the landscape, most of us can recognize only a few of them at a glance and only in a general sort of way. We know a pine, for instance, when we see one, or an oak or a maple or birch, but can we distin-

ADVENTURE 30

We Consider Some Diagnostic Characters

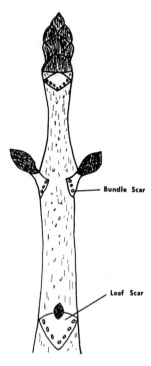

Bundle Scar

Leaf Scar

Figure 121
TWIG OF HORSE CHESTNUT

guish between a white pine and a pitch pine, between a white oak and a red oak, or between a silver maple and a sugar maple?

Most of our trees are easy to identify once you have learned how. It is much like getting to know people you meet. Once you have met them, you recognize them the next time by certain characteristics, as the color of the hair or eyes, the shape of the mouth or nose, or by other features. We can know our trees in much the same way.

The best time of the year to study them is in the winter. Most of our trees have a distinct shape or form that is more or less hidden in the foliage of summer, but when they stand naked and silhouetted against the sky, it is then that their architectural contours are most perfectly revealed and their natural grace and beauty most clearly defined. Once you have seen the umbrella or vaselike form of the American elm outlined against the winter's sky, you will never forget it. Nor will you forget the pin oak, with its tall straight trunk and pyramidal head, or the Lombardy poplar, which looks like a church steeple. All of our trees do not have such distinct or characteristic forms. All do, however, have twig structures we can use to identify them. These structures are called diagnostic characters.

Examine the twig of any tree after the

leaves have fallen, for instance the horse chestnut illustrated in *Figure 121*. Observe the smooth, light-colored areas that appear at first glance as scars. And that is exactly what they are—leaf scars, formed when the leaves fall off. The shedding of leaves when cold weather approaches is nature's way of protecting the trees against excessive loss of water during the winter, when the supply is at a minimum and it becomes necessary for every tree to conserve whatever it can obtain from the soil. Leaves function, in addition to their food-making activities, as an outlet for any excess water that the trees may absorb from the soil, at such times as when the water table is high, and that, if not eliminated, would drown them. Since the leaves would continue to function in this manner, were they permitted to remain on the twigs during the winter, it is quite possible that the outgo of water might exceed the intake, with resultant injury to the trees. The subject of leaf fall is physiologically an interesting one and more complicated than we can discuss here.

Most leaf scars are visible to the naked eye, but in some cases we need our lens to outline them clearly. Look at your leaf scars with the lens and you will see small raised dots. These dots, called bundle scars, indicate the ends of the conducting vessels that carried water in

Figure 122
LEAF SCAR OF RED MAPLE

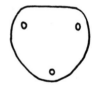

Figure 123
LEAF SCAR OF AMERICAN ELM

and out of the leaves. As you probably know, the water entering the leaves carries dissolved minerals for food-making, and on leaving the leaves carries dissolved food materials, which are carried to all parts of the plant and used or stored as the occasion may require. The shape of the leaf scars and the number and arrangement of the bundle scars vary in different trees, but are always constant for each species.

Let us consider the twig of the horse chestnut, a fairly common tree in our cities and towns. The leaf scars are very large and may easily be seen with the naked eye. Observe that they are inversely triangular (*Figure 121*) and that they are arranged opposite one another on the twig. Note also that there are seven bundle scars also visible to the naked eye and that they are arranged in a simple curved line. Now let us compare this twig with one from the red maple. Observe, first of all, that the twigs differ markedly in size. The leaf scars and bundle scars, as might be expected, also differ in this respect. But not only do they differ in size; they differ in other respects. The leaf scars in the red maple are not triangular, as in the horse chestnut, but broad, U-shaped (*Figure 122*), and the bundle scars are only three in number. The leaf scars are arranged oppositely as in the horse chestnut.

We next examine a twig of the American elm and note first of all that the leaf scars are arranged alternately on the twig. Then that they are semicircular in outline. If we now look closely at them with our lens, we observe that they are slightly raised above the surface of the twig and that, though small, they are fairly conspicuous because of the contrast in color between the light, corky surface of the scar and the darker brown of the twig. The bundle scars are three in number and rather large and noticeable *(Figure 123)*.

These three examples serve to illustrate the degree of variation we might expect to find in these characters. Leaf scars may have almost any form and in addition to those we have just discussed may be circular and crescent-shaped. They may be very narrow, as in the pear, and their upper margins may be flat, convex, as in the black ash *(Figure 124)*, or deeply notched, as in the white ash *(Figure 125)*. Sometimes they may form a band nearly surrounding the bud, as in the sycamore. In some cases they may be dingy and inconspicuous or be quite distinct by reason of a color contrast, as in the elm, which we have mentioned. They may be level with the twig or more or less raised, with their surface parallel with the twig or making various angles with it up to a right angle. Much the same can be said of the bundle scars in regard

Figure 124
LEAF SCAR OF BLACK ASH

Figure 125
LEAF SCAR OF WHITE ASH

to their number, size, relation to the surface of the leaf scar, as sunken or projecting, and their arrangement.

Though there may be many variations in these structures, the structures themselves, as we have already remarked, are fairly constant for the species, and as you pursue this study and examine the twigs of our trees, you will gradually associate certain characters with certain species. Thus the large triangular leaf scar, with its seven bundle scars arranged in a single curved line, is characteristic of the horse chestnut; the U-shaped leaf scar, with its three bundle scars, we associate with the red maple; and so on. You might begin your study by collecting twigs from the trees in your neighborhood, and then, with the aid of a book on trees, identify, label, and keep them for ready reference.

ADVENTURE 31

We Inspect the Breathing Apparatus of Some Aquatic Insects

EVERY LIVING PLANT and animal needs air, or, more specifically, oxygen, to live. Oxygen is necessary for respiration, a word applied to a number of complex chemical processes whereby food materials are converted, among other products, into heat and energy. In many animals, as birds and mammals, oxygen as a component of air passes directly into the body, where the lungs effect a transfer of the oxygen from the air into the blood stream; in other animals, as fishes, the gills effect a transfer of oxygen from water into the blood stream.

Insects have neither lungs nor gills. Instead they have a network of tubes called tracheae and smaller tubes called tracheoles, which convey air to the remotest tissues of the body. The tracheae are provided with openings to the exterior through which air enters, as in our nostrils. These openings are called spiracles and, with a hand lens, are easily visible on the abdominal segments (of the grasshopper, for instance).

This kind of respiratory system does very well for terrestrial or land insects, but how about those that live in water? Would not the water enter through the spiracles and then course throughout the tracheal system and drown them, much as water would enter our nostrils and into our lungs if we submerged and remained beneath the surface for any length of time? Aquatic insects, however, have developed modifications of the tracheal system that enable them to live in water.

Between the terrestrial insects and those which are truly aquatic is a group of insects that can be referred to as semi-aquatic. They dwell, for the most part, on or near the surface of the water and, being air breathers, submerge for only rather short periods. All have tracheal systems with open spiracles. In this group belong such insects as the water striders, which we often see skimming over the surface of a pond, and the whirligig beetles, the little blue, oval-shaped, metallic-appearing beetles that swim about in circles in the quiet parts of a pond or stream. Also in the group are such insects as the diving beetles, watch boatmen, back swimmers, water scorpions, rat-tailed maggots, and mosquito larvae and pupae, which are found usually beneath the surface. But they are not truly aquatic forms, since they are air breathers. How, then, do they obtain air?

Some of them, as the diving beetles, water boatmen, and back swimmers, periodically rise to the surface to breathe in the normal manner, and when they dive carry down bubbles of air, which permit them to remain submerged for varying periods. When the air supply is exhausted they rise to the surface. The others, as the water scorpions, rat-tailed maggots, and the larvae and pupae of mosquitoes, are provided with special breathing tubes, which they extend above the surface of the water. The various adaptations exhibited by these and other semi-aquatic insects, not alone for respiration, but for living in an aquatic habitat, makes for the most interesting reading. We are not concerned with

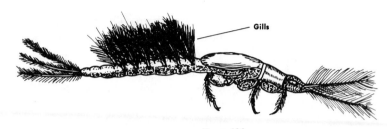

Figure 126

MAY-FLY NYMPH

these insects, however, except in passing, but rather with the truly aquatic species and the means they have developed for obtaining oxygen.

In the truly aquatic insects, which are essentially immature forms as nymphs and larvae and which live beneath the surface, the spiracles have become suppressed or functionless, and respiration is effected by means of gills. These gills are hairlike or platelike expansions of the body wall and are abundantly supplied with tracheae and tracheoles. Hence they are known as tracheal gills. They are so thin that oxygen can pass from water through their walls into the tracheae and thence into the body. Many May-fly nymphs (*Figure 126*) have leaflike gills in which the tracheal system is clearly visible with a hand lens. These nymphs live in clean fresh water, flowing rivulets or rivers, tumbling waterfalls or quiet pools, and usually we have no trouble collecting them. They may best be collected with a pan or some sort of scoop or a water net dragged slowly over the bottom along the shore of a pond, river, or pool where the water is shallow. May-fly nymphs vary in size and shape, but they all agree in having seven pairs of gills on the abdomen and two or three long slender tail filaments. The gills, when examined with a lens, appear as in *Figure 127*.

Although tracheal gills are usually located on the abdomen, as in the May flies, dobson flies, and caddis flies, they are sometimes located on the head and thorax, as in the stone flies. In the dragonflies they are found in the rectum at the posterior part of the body and are known as rectal gills, and in the related damsel flies they take the form of three flat plates at the posterior end of the body and hence are known as caudal gills (*Figure 128*). The gills of the damsel flies are bathed by water drawn into the rectum and expelled at rather irregular intervals. Should you place one of these damsel flies in a container of water, a pan, for instance, you may find that it will turn over on its back with its legs bent double, and while thus "playing dead" suddenly be propelled forward by the expulsion of a stream of water from the tracheal chamber.

Adult May flies usually appear in May and

Figure 127
TRACHEAL GILLS OF MAY FLY

may be seen then in swarms in the vicinity of streams, ponds, and lakes. Frequently the banks are strewn with their dead bodies. They are attracted to lights and it is not uncommon to see hundreds of them about a street light. These insects are also known as ephemerids, a word derived from the Greek *ephemeros,* which means "lasting but a day." It has reference to the fact that the adult May flies are short-lived. They live usually only a single day or night or but a few hours, though sometimes they may live a few days. The name, however, is misleading, for though the adults live only a short time, the nymphs may live as long as three years before they transform. The insects are an interesting group and present some curious features. One of these is the complete absence of mouth parts in the adults, as you can readily see by examining them with your lens. This explains their short span of life as adults, since they cannot eat. Another curious sidelight is that, unlike other insects, the May flies molt after they have obtained functional wings.

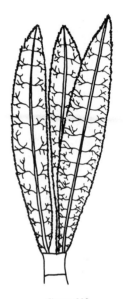

Figure 128
CAUDAL GILLS OF DAMSELFLY

LET US LOOK at a fish scale, or rather a few of them, for they are not all alike. Indeed, like other things we have already discussed in previous Adventures, they differ in ap-

ADVENTURE 32

*We Do
Some Fishing*

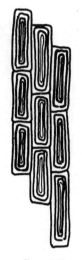

Figure 129
GANOID SCALE

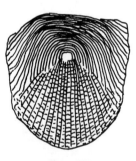

Figure 130
CYCLOID SCALE OF
COMMON SHINER

pearance and form according to the species, and here again we have another illustration of variation so characteristic of nature's workings.

First of all, what purpose do they serve, and, second, what are they? They form the outer protective covering of the fish and are formed by certain scale-forming cells in the dermis. These cells lay down two layers of different substance, an outer layer, which is bony, and an inner layer, which is fibrillar or threadlike with calcareous deposits. As the fish grows the scales increase in thickness and size by successive additions of bony material, these additions being indicated by lines of growth. As periods of growth alternate with periods of comparative inactivity, due to seasonal variation in food, it is possible for us to estimate the relative age of a fish by examining these diary-like lines.

There are three principal types of scales: ganoid, cycloid, and ctenoid. Ganoid scales (*Figure 129*) are usually rhomboid or diamond shape, and occur in such fishes as the gars, pikes, and sturgeons. Cycloid scales (*Figure 130*) are usually circular, with concentric rings about a central point, and are found in the trout, minnows, and most other soft-rayed fishes. Ctenoid scales (*Figure 131*), which are characteristic of the perch, bass, sunfish, and most other spiny-rayed fishes are similar to cycloid scales except that the posterior margin bears small spines or teeth. Both of these two types of scales are arranged in overlapping rows like the shingles of a house.

Now examine some scales with our lens. The question arises, where to get them? We can get them at any fish market or catch our own fish. A scale may be removed from a fish with a knife or pair of forceps (tweezers), and it isn't necessary to kill the fish to do so. Indeed, after a scale has been removed the fish may be replaced in the water.

Everyone who has fished in our ponds and streams knows the sunfish, a beautiful and gamy little fish (*Figure 132*), an inhabitant of almost every pond throughout the Eastern and Central states. Another fish, equally well known and abundant in almost every pond and small stream east of the Rocky Mountains, is the common shiner (*Figure 130*). The yellow perch, too, is familiar (*Figure 131*). Lastly, the brook trout needs no introduction (*Figure 133*).

If you decide to get your scales from your fish market, ask your fish dealer to save some scales for you the next time he cleans fish. If he is a co-operative sort of fellow, perhaps you can get him to put the scales in small separate envelopes and mark each envelope with the name of the fish from which the enclosed scales were removed. You should, of

Figure 131
CTENOID SCALE OF YELLOW PERCH

Figure 132
SCALE OF SUNFISH

Figure 133
SCALE OF BROOK TROUT

course, supply him with the envelopes. Should you care to keep scales as a permanent collection, it is advisable to clean them. Be careful not to break the margin of the scales or to disrupt the soft inner surfaces. After they have been thoroughly çleaned, put them aside to dry, then mount them on small cards and label.

ADVENTURE 33

We Turn Our Attention to Buds

In ADVENTURE 30 we became acquainted with leaf scars and bundle scars and found that they help us to identify trees and shrubs, especially in winter. Buds, too, serve the same purpose.

Most of us think of buds as unopened or unexpanded flowers, but this is only partially right, for there are buds that produce stem growth and leaves. The buds we find on twigs and branches of trees and shrubs are rudimentary stems and consist of a short length of partially developed stems with leaves in various stages of development. We can see this for ourselves if we cut a bud transversely and examine it with our lens. A bud of the cottonwood cut in this manner is shown in *Figure 134*.

Buds of trees and shrubs are usually protected by several layers of overlapping scales, called bud scales, which are really modified

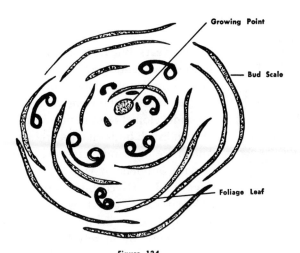

Figure 134
CROSS SECTION OF
COTTONWOOD LEAF BUD

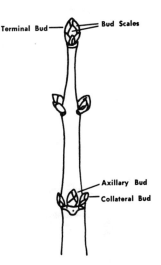

Figure 135
TWIG OF RED MAPLE

leaves (*Figure 135*). These bud scales are often covered with hair, as in the willow, and sometimes, as in the cottonwood, with a waxy secretion effective in protecting the enclosed tender structures from drying out and from mechanical injury. In the woody plants of the moist tropics and in herbaceous plants the buds are not protected by scales and are said to be naked.

Buds found on the twigs and branches of trees and shrubs are formed during the summer of the preceding year and are known as winter buds, since they live through this part

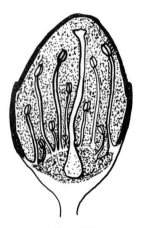

Figure 136
LONGITUDINAL SECTION OF
FRUIT BUD

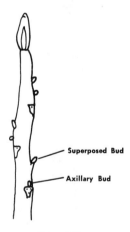

Superposed Bud

Axillary Bud

Figure 137
TWIG OF BUTTERNUT

of the year. Buds are known as leaf buds, flower buds, and mixed buds. Leaf buds contain a number of small or undeveloped leaves. Flower buds contain one or more miniature or undeveloped flowers but no foliage leaves. We find such buds on fruit trees, for instance, and if we open one lengthwise and examine it with our lens, it will appear as shown in *Figure 136*. Mixed buds contain both undeveloped leaves and flowers. As a rule it is not possible to distinguish leaf buds from flower buds by merely looking at them, although in some cases, as in the elm, the flower buds are larger.

In tree identification the position or arrangement of the buds on a twig is considered. Buds found on the end of stems are known as terminal buds (*Figure 135*). Axillary buds (*Figure 135*) develop in the leaf axils, which are places on the stem directly above where the leaves are attached. Frequently other buds are found in company with these axillary buds. They are called accessory buds and may be either superposed (*Figure 137*) or collateral (*Figure 135*). Lastly there are buds that are formed anywhere on the stem except at the tip and leaf axils. They are the so-called adventitious buds.

Variations occur among buds as in other plant structures. These variations, as shape, number of scales, presence or absence of hairs, etc., may seem insignificant, yet they are constant for the species. After a while you will associate certain kinds of buds with specific trees and shrubs, and tree identification will be almost a perfunctory habit.

We have discussed buds—now let us look at a few of them as a sort of practice exercise. We shall select first the Norway maple, which has been planted extensively as a shade tree and thus should be available. The buds, which are rather large for a maple, are commonly red or yellowish green toward the base, and sometimes the entire bud is strongly tinged with green. The terminal bud is larger than the lateral buds, oval or ovate in shape. In comparison the lateral buds are small and appressed, that is, they lie close against the twig (*Figure 138*). We can see all this with the naked eye. With our lens we now examine the bud scales and observe that they are more or less keeled, or with a ridge like the keel of a boat, and that the margins are covered with fine hairs. We next count the scales of the terminal bud. To find them all, we must lift up some of the scales with a pin. There are five pairs. The enclosed scales are covered with dark, rusty-brown hairs.

For our second choice we find ourselves in something of a dilemma. Since some of you live in the city and others in the country, the same trees may not be available to everyone,

Figure 138
TWIG OF NORWAY MAPLE

Figure 139
TWIG OF SUGAR MAPLE

Figure 140
TWIG OF ASPEN

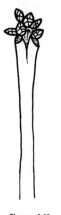

Figure 141
TWIG OF WHITE OAK

so let us take an imaginary walk. As we leave our house our attention is attracted to a rather stately tree growing by the roadside. We look at the buds and find that they are conical to ovate (egg-shaped) in form and sharply pointed. They are also reddish in color. Using our lens to examine them more closely, we also find that they are rather downy, especially toward the tip. If we next count the scales, we find four to eight overlapping pairs with margins finely hairy (*Figure 139*). The tree is the sugar maple.

We continue on and after we have gone a short distance we observe a tree with a light green bark. We pause and look at the buds, which we find to be of two shapes and sizes. Some are narrowly conical and very sharply pointed; others are ovate and larger. All lie close to the twig and are shining; indeed, they appear sticky, and when we touch them we find that they are. When we look at the scales with our lens, we note that they are reddish brown and rather thin and dry along the margins (*Figure 140*). The tree is the aspen, and the larger, ovate buds are flower buds.

Not far from the aspen is a tree whose light gray or nearly white bark appears broken by fissures into long, irregular, thin scales. Anxious to examine it more closely, we go over, and, looking at the twigs, we observe that the buds are clustered at the ends of the twigs (*Figure 141*). The buds themselves are broadly ovate and blunt, and when we look at them with our lens we observe that they are somewhat five-sided, with five rows of closely overlapping, reddish-brown scales. Buds clustered at the ends of the twigs are a characteristic of oaks, and from the color of the white bark we label this tree the white oak.

The next buds we examine are quite unlike anything we have seen thus far. They are stout, semi-spherical, rusty to dark brown, and a few are even black. Through the lens they are more or less downy. The scales of the terminal bud are in opposite pairs with sharply abrupt points (*Figure 142*). The buds identify the tree as the white ash.

Leaving the white ash, we wander about and suddenly discover that we are in a wet field, and here we see a tree with slender yellowish buds that, beneath our lens, appear to be crowded with glandular dots. As we look carefully we observe that the buds are slightly hairy between the scales (*Figure 143*). We also observe that the scales, strangely, do not overlap. In botanical terminology they are said to be valvate. These odd-shaped buds belong to the bitternut, a member of the hickory family.

The wet field merges into a moist wood-

Figure 142
TWIG OF WHITE ASH

Figure 143
TWIG OF BITTERNUT

land, the natural habitat of the red maple, often called the swamp maple. This tree is very well named, for some part of it is red in every season of the year. The twigs and buds are red and prove a pleasant contrast to the white landscape of winter; the flowers are red in spring and so are the fruits that follow; and in the fall the leaves flash a brilliant red against the blue October sky. The buds are bluntly pointed and vary from oval-ovate to spherical, with four pairs of scales. As we study the twigs we see the presence of collateral buds (*Figure 135*). These buds, as you may remember, are buds that occur on either side of the axillary buds.

There are many other trees whose buds we can examine on our imaginary walk, but these examples should serve to illustrate the use of buds in tree identification. Whether you continue with this subject, which can be a very fascinating one, is for you to decide. But should you stop here, at least you will have discovered that buds are not necessarily the prosaic things most people consider them to be.

ADVENTURE 34

*We Trace
Some Tunnels*

UNLESS YOU KNOW SOMETHING about entomology, you may wonder what leaf miners are. Go outdoors with your hand lens—into the garden or neighboring field—assuming it is summer, and look for a leaf with blotches (*Figure 144*) or twisting lines (*Figure 145*)—leaves with these disfigurements are common. Remove the leaf from its stem and hold it up so the light will pass through it. You should find the blotch or twisted line occupied by a small, wormlike creature, unless the little animal has reached maturity and been transformed into an adult insect, when it would have left its temporary home and taken up a different kind of existence.

The twisting lines and blotches are passages or tunnels that the larvae of certain insects excavate in the tissues of the leaves. The insects may be beetles, flies, moths, or sawflies, but despite their diversity as insects they all have one thing in common—small size. It seems incredible that some insects are so small that they are able to live between the upper and lower surfaces of a leaf that is almost of paper thinness. Not only can they live there, but they manage to grow and increase in size. This is indicated by the increasing width of the passageways. Follow one of these twisting passageways from the beginning. Note that it begins almost as a pinpoint, and here is where the egg hatched. You will see that it becomes progressively wider and wider.

There are two general types of mines, as the blotches and tunnels are known: the

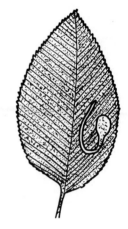

Figure 144
MINE OF ELM-LEAF MINER

Figure 145
MINE OF COLUMBINE-LEAF MINER

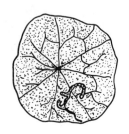

twisting, or linear, mine made by the insect as it moved forward, and the round, or blotch, mine made by the insect as it moved around and around within the leaf. There are many modifications of these two types as the linear-blotch, the trumpet, the digitate, and the tentiform. Indeed, the patterns described by the insects as they eat their way through the plant tissues may be as varied as the insects themselves. But each species makes its own characteristic design, so that anyone familiar with these insects can usually identify the species merely by looking at the form of the mine. As one writer has put it, "they write their signatures on the leaves."

Even though the leaf miners are provided with shelter and plenty of food, they do not live an altogether carefree existence. Like anyone else, they too have their problems. Sometimes they find the veins of the leaves a barrier to further progress, and they must either eat through them or confine their operations to a limited area. They must be careful, too, not to cut the latex cells lest the secretions from these cells pour into their mines and drown them. But their gravest problem is waste disposal. Some miners distribute the wastes over the floor of the mine, as you can see with your lens, while others go to the trouble of excavating side chambers in which to dispose of their refuse. Still others have developed the habit of cutting holes in the surface of the leaf through which they push out their fecula, which is the accepted term for the waste material or excrement voided by insects.

A common leaf miner is a small fly whose larva makes a kind of twisting tunnel, called a serpentine mine, in the leaf of the columbine (*Figure 145*). The columbine is a favorite perennial of most gardeners, and you should have no difficulty finding it. Observe that the mine is a whitish tortuous or twisting trail that frequently crosses itself and finally ends in a spot about an eighth of an inch wide. Here is where the maggot pupated and transformed into the adult. The nasturtium is another garden plant frequently inhabited by a leaf miner (*Figure 146*). Even a pine needle may have its little inhabitant— the pine-leaf miner. If you can find a pine needle with its occupant and hold it up to the light, you may observe the little creature running up and down in its tunnel as if it were dismayed at being disturbed (*Figure 147*). Note a small hole near the lower end of the tunnel. This hole is where the larva entered the leaf and through which, after it has enlarged it slightly, it will emerge as an adult.

Leaf miners attack nearly all families of plants and some of them are quite destructive. Frequently an entire family may occupy

Figure 147
MINE OF PINE-LEAF MINER

a leaf, and if you hold such a leaf up to the light, you will find that each member makes its own little niche, all eventually joining together to make one large blotch or blister.

In Adventure 29 we learned something about minerals and we looked at several of the common ones. Let us go a little further afield and get acquainted with a few more.

Minerals are where you find them. There are localities where certain minerals occur in abundance, but we aren't all able to visit them, nor is it necessary to do so. As many minerals occur in rocks, we need only to look for rocks. Bare and exposed rocks, where fresh and unweathered surfaces are available, are often productive. Quarries and places where crushed stone is made are excellent sites. It is just a matter of grubbing around and examining them at random. It is advisable, however, and often necessary, to get permission from an authorized official of the company before you are allowed to explore their workings. Permission is usually granted with the warning not to get too close to the bottom of the cliffs.

Other likely sites are places where blasting has occurred in road construction. Fissures and cavities in cliffs or ledges or large boulders should be explored, for they frequently contain fine crystals. All you will need for equipment is your lens and a hammer, preferably a stonemason's hammer, for breaking up the rocks. A pair of thick-soled shoes will make walking among the rocks somewhat more comfortable, and unless you want to stuff your pockets, take a bag or box in which to carry home your specimens. I might add that if you are really interested in looking for minerals it would pay you to locate someone who is either an amateur or professional mineralogist and write for a list of localities in your state where specific minerals occur. Colleges and universities that have a mineralogy department have such lists and would be glad to give one to you.

You have doubtless heard of fool's gold. This is one of our commonest minerals and one you should have no trouble finding. It occurs in all kinds of rocks in the form of cubes, octahedrons, and pyritohedrons (*Figure 148*), terms that need not concern you too much. You will readily recognize it by its brassy color and metallic luster. As a mineral, it is known as pyrite. It is a compound of iron and sulphur and though very abundant is rarely used as a source of iron because the sulphur is difficult to remove and to leave it in the iron would make the latter brittle and useless for most purposes.

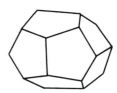

Figure 148
PYRITOHEDRON CRYSTAL OF PYRITE

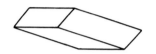

Calcite is another very common and abundant mineral and, since it is usually colorless or white, is easily found. It occurs in well-defined crystals, but the form of the crystals varies considerably. All the forms, however, are variations of the rhombohedron (*Figure 149*). Should you ever be in doubt as to the identity of a calcite specimen, place a drop of hydrochloric acid on it. If calcite it will effervesce, or fizz. Calcite is a carbonate of calcium and is soluble in water. This is the material that mollusks, corals, echinoderms, and other animals take from the water to make their shells and other more or less permanent structures in which they live.

As I write I have before me on my desk a rock about six inches in diameter which I found on one of my collecting trips. Embedded in it are a number of garnet crystals. Garnet occurs usually either in the form of a dodecahedron (*Figure 150*) or a trapezohedron and is found essentially in metamorphic rocks but is also present in other kinds of rocks. It occurs in various tints of red, brown, yellow, green, and occasionally black and in size ranges from that of a grain of sand to that of a marble; sometimes garnets may be found as large as four inches in diameter. The ones I have are yellowish and are found throughout New England and the

Piedmont Plateau. Garnet is usually crushed and used as an abrasive, especially for finishing wood and leather, but pure and clear specimens are frequently used as gems. I also have a specimen of tourmaline on my desk. This is not a common mineral and may be found only in certain localities; hence the need for a list of localities. This mineral may easily be recognized by its black or brown color and its three-sided prismatic crystals (*Figure 151*).

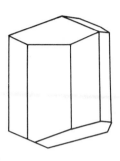

Figure 151
PRISMATIC CRYSTAL OF TOURMALINE

Galena, which is a compound of lead, is a mineral found in every state in the Union and is usually associated with pyrite and calcite. Be on the watch for it when you find specimens of these two minerals. It is lead gray in color, with a metallic luster, and occurs in well-formed cubic crystals. Beryl is another mineral that is fairly common in certain rocks. It is usually some tint of green and occurs in hexagonal crystals (*Figure 152*). A specimen free from cracks and inclosures and of gem quality is so rare that its value is greater than that of the diamond. We know it as the emerald.

No matter where you look you are sure to find the mineral limonite, for it is nothing more than iron rust. It does not occur in the crystal form, but in masses and incrustations. A brown stain on a rock is sure to be limonite.

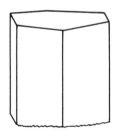

Figure 152
HEXAGONAL CRYSTAL OF BERYL

The mineral is not an important source of iron; its chief use is as a pigment (ocher yellow) for paints.

The chief source of iron is the mineral hematite, found everywhere, in some states in considerable deposits. Hematite occurs as small crystals and in masses. You will most likely find it in the non-crystalline form in rocks where its red color will call it to your attention.

ADVENTURE 36

We Scrutinize a Miniature Pepper Box

AN INDIVIDUAL MOSS PLANT is a rather inconspicuous form of vegetation, and yet when a number of them are found growing together they collectively provide a bit of greenery to places that would otherwise appear drab and barren. They cover the woodland floor with a soft green carpet and are the first plants to appear on the naked sides of ditches, clay banks, and other unsightly spots. As little cushions they fill in the crevices of pavements and relieve the harshness of rocks and boulders. A decaying log is never so attractive as when it is covered with mosses and lichens.

The leafy moss plant in itself may not be of much interest except to those who have discovered an interesting hobby in the study of the mosses. But the spore cases are another matter, since they are somewhat unique in themselves and provide a further illustration of variation, which we find so prevalent in all of nature's wonders.

For our purpose we shall select the spore case of the hairy-cap moss because this is one of the most abundant as well as one of the largest of the mosses. The hairy-cap grows in dry fields and meadows and on dry knolls and near the margins of damp woodlands. Like other mosses it is subject to great extremes of moisture and dryness and differs in appearance under varying conditions. During a period of dry weather the leaves fold up lengthwise and twist into the merest threads, so that the soft green surfaces will expose the least area to the air and thus prevent loss of water through evaporation. With a rain or return of moisture they straighten out and are again green and leaflike.

The spore cases of the hairy-cap may be found only during the months of June and July. We then find them perched at the tips of stiff, ruddy little stalks that rise into the air from among the leaves (*Figure 153*). When we look at one of these spore cases through our lens, we observe first of all that it is covered with a yellowish mohair cap, ending in a golden-brown peak at its tip (*Figure 153*). This cap, or calyptra, as it is called, was present from the very moment the

Calyptra

Figure 153
HAIRY CAP MOSS

Figure 154
CAPSULE OF HAIRY CAP MOSS

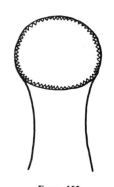

Figure 155
PERISTOME OF A MOSS

spore case started to form, and served as a protective covering for the delicate tissues throughout its development. We can lift it off very easily and expose the spore case, or capsule. It is a beautiful green object, four-sided or cubical in shape, with a lid (operculum) on top like a sugar-bowl cover except that it has a point instead of a knob at its center (*Figure 154*).

We next pry off the lid with a sharp knife and look at the uncovered end with our lens. We see a row of tiny teeth (peristome) around the margin (*Figure 155*) and if we count them carefully we find that there are sixty-four of them. Between the teeth we note small openings, and it is through these openings that the spores escape when ripe. The capsule is in fact a miniature pepper box, with a grating around its upper edge instead of holes in the cover.

As we look at a clump of hairy-caps we observe that some capsules are held in a vertical position, while others are held horizontally. Here we have an interesting provision. Until the spores are mature, the capsule is held vertically, but when the spores are ready to be released the capsule is moved through an angle of ninety degrees so that the spores may more easily be shaken out. The teeth also illustrate another interesting habit. They behave much like the leaves; when moist they swell and close up the openings between them. The reason for this is to prevent the spores from falling out in wet weather, when they would fall to the ground among the parent plants, where there is little room for them to develop into new plants. In dry weather the wind scatters them to places where they would likely find more favorable conditions.

Capsules of mosses may be found at almost any time of the year, since the many species do not all mature their spores at the same time. Examine them whenever you find them and you will discover that some are round, others are cylindrical, while still others are curved. You will also find that the number of teeth vary and that the teeth may be entire or split or irregular, and in some instances there is a double row of them. There are countless variations, and for those who are interested in these plants they help in identification.

GALLS ARE the strange and eye-catching outgrowths or excrescences so common on plants. These odd structures, formed mostly by insects, occur in a variety of shapes and sizes. Some are only blister-like swellings on the leaves, while others are hairy or pile-like

ADVENTURE 37

We Invade the Privacy of Gall Makers

growths. Others are suggestive of bullets, and some take a spherical form as much as an inch or more in diameter. Then there are various deformations of stems and roots, often in grotesque shapes, and aborted flowers and flower clusters that appear as if ravaged by some terrible disease. The habit of gall formation is believed to have been the first insect habit observed by man, although it was not known for a long time that insects were responsible for these outgrowths. Pliny writes about them and Theophrastus refers to their medical and curative properties. Both of these men lived some two thousand years ago but it was not until 1686 that Malpighi, a physician and botanist, in a treatise called *De Gallis,* explained what causes them.

There are probably more than fifteen hundred different kinds of galls. The number is unimportant—of more interest is what they are, how they are produced, and their economic value. Strangely enough, in spite of their apparent worthlessness, many of them have found application in the arts and sciences. Tannic acid is one of the chief products. Various dyes are obtained from certain species. Permanent inks have for years been made from them. Some galls have been used in medicine and upon occasion as food—a gall found in the Near East has been an article of commerce, and in Missouri and Arkansas an oak gall is fed, when abundant, to cattle, hogs, and sheep, as well as to chickens and turkeys, with excellent results.

Galls occur on almost every form of plant life and may be found on any part of a plant —root, branch, leaf, blossom, fruit, and even seed—in fact, on any part that furnishes food to the gall maker. Some galls are very simple in structure; others are most complicated. Many are highly attractive and striking in form and coloration. There is no evidence that the form is of any adaptive importance, and the answer may be that the formation of any specific form is purely mechanical. But the remarkable feature about galls is that those made by the same species of insect are all of the same form, are all formed on the same species of plant, and are always on the same part of the plant, so that those versed in gall lore may know the identity of the gall maker by merely looking at the gall.

Although we know that galls are produced by insects—and in some instances also by mites and nematode worms—we still do not know what causes them or just how they are produced. It is generally believed that the formation of a gall is initiated, or that the plant tissues are stimulated in growing abnormally, by a secretion from the larva. Yet the fact remains that the physiology of gall formation is still obscure. The study of galls is a fascinating one, and the study of the insects that make them is, in some respects, difficult, for we cannot always be sure that the insect that emerges from the gall is the one that made it, since many insects do not make galls but lay their eggs in those made by others. Such insects are called "guests." Furthermore, both the makers and the guests are attacked by parasitic bees and wasps, which only adds to our confusion, for it is not always easy to determine the interrelations of these insects. Many galls are complicated communities. In one case as many as thirty different kinds of insects, belonging to almost all the orders, were reared from a single species of gall.

Galls are especially numerous on willows, oaks, roses, legumes, and composites, so we should have no difficulty finding them. One of the most common and abundant is the so-called oak apple. Occasionally oak apples are so numerous as to suggest a fair crop of fruit on an apple tree. They are globular in shape and the larger ones an inch or two in diameter. They appear in May or June, and as we first look at them they seem to grow directly from the bud, but on closer inspection we note that each oak apple is a deformed leaf. If we cut one open with a sharp knife or razor blade when it is still in the process of being formed and examine it with

Figure 156
OAK APPLE

our lens, we shall probably find internally a juicy, spongy white substance and a large central larval cell containing a small grub or young gall wasp (*Figure 156*). There are different kinds of oak apples, and if we selected one that is green with red spots and opened it, we would find that instead of a spongy substance supporting the larval cell it is supported by radiating fibers (*Figure 157*). The occupant, as before, is also a gall wasp.

An extremely beautiful gall, indeed one of the most beautiful objects in nature, is the wool-sower (*Figure 158*). It occurs on the twigs of various oaks, is woolly creamy white, and is admirably set off with pinkish-red blotches, the woolly growth with seedlike grains. Here is really an object for your lens.

There are so many different kinds of galls that I find it difficult to know which to describe or which to suggest that you examine. Perhaps it is best you look for them yourself. Do not expect to find the gall maker in its dwelling once it has become an adult, for it then has no longer any need for a shelter and will have left it. You can always tell whether the occupant has left by a small exit hole. If you want to find the maker still within its little home, open only those galls that are still fresh-looking and not the brown dried ones, although in some cases such galls may contain the hibernating occupants, as there

Figure 157
OAK APPLE

Figure 158
WOOL-SOWER

Figure 159
GOLDENROD GALL

Figure 160
GOLDENROD GALL SHOWING
HIBERNATING LARVA

are some gall makers that use their shelters for winter retreats. Three such galls come to mind, two of which are found on goldenrod stems. One is oval (*Figure 159*) and provides a winter home for the larva of a moth, and the other is spherical (*Figure 160*) and serves as the hibernaculum for the larva of a fly. Both may be found in midwinter. The third is the pine cone willow gall (*Figure 161*), shaped like a pine cone and formed on the terminal buds of willow stems by the gall gnat. It is very common and there are often dozens of them on one willow. An interesting facet of this gall is that it often shelters a number of insect guests. As many as thirty-one dwellers have been listed as occupying one of these galls at one time, in addition to its maker. Open one and see how many insects you can find and how many different species they represent.

ADVENTURE 38

We Are Introduced to Some Queer Plants

In early spring we often notice queer, pale-colored plants that shoot up above the ground in sandy and gravelly places, as along the roadside, in a waste place, and along a railway embankment. These plants are called horsetails, possibly because of the fancied resemblance to a horse's tail of the green vegetative shoots that follow later. They are of no economic value today, but if we can judge from the fossil remains, which show a considerable number and variety of these plants, they probably were at one time an important element in the flora of the earth, like the ferns, and contributed their vegetative parts and spores to the formation of coal during the Carboniferous Period.

As we look closely at one of these plants, we observe that the stalk is pale and rather weird in appearance (*Figure 162*). The stem, which is the same diameter from bottom to top, is ornamented at intervals with slender, black, pointed scales. These scales, which point upward, are united at the bottom and encircle the stalk in a slightly bulging ring which shows a ridge for every scale, extending down the stem. The scales are much-reduced leaves that long ago lost the ability to carry on photosynthesis, the process by which green plants manufacture their food materials from the water of the soil and carbon dioxide of the air.

Continuing our examination of the plant, we note further that the tip is surmounted by a cone-shaped whitish structure called a strobilus. If we look at it through our lens we find that it is made up of tiny disks that remind us of miniature toadstools. On the lower surface

Figure 161
PINE CONE WILLOW GALL

— Strobilus

Figure 162
FERTILE UNCOLORED SHOOT OF HORSETAIL

Figure 163
SPORANGIUM OF HORSETAIL

Figure 164
STERILE GREEN
SHOOT OF HORSETAIL

of each disk can be seen from five to ten sacs that are spore-producing structures, or sporangia (*Figure 163*). After the spores have been released, these sporangia hang around the disk in torn scallops.

The spore-producing shoot is only part of the horsetail plant. As soon as the spores have been released, the shoot dies down and is followed by a slender green shoot with numerous branches set in whorls at intervals, or nodes (*Figure 164*). At one time the plant probably had a whorl of leaves at each node, but since there are now so many green branches, the leaves have been reduced to mere points and appear to be merely a sort of trimming. Each little cup or socket of the joint or node, in branch or stem, has a row of points around its margin. If a branch is triangular in cross-section, it will have three points, if quadrangular, four points, and so on. Both the stem and branches are made up entirely of segments, each set at its lower end in the socket of the segment below it and each easily pulled out.

As you handle the horsetails you will find that they are rough and of harsh texture. The reason for this is that they are impregnated with silica, and on this account the plant was formerly used for cleaning and polishing metal utensils and was given the name "scouring rush."

In Adventure 21 we discussed the eggs of the lacewing. You may recall that each egg was placed at the tip of a stalk to prevent the other eggs from being eaten by an emerging aphis lion. I remarked at the time that this shows an interesting provision, and so it does, but it is a departure from the normal egg-laying habits of insects and should not be accepted as typical. Most insects need not be concerned that their eggs will be eaten by hatching young, so they lay their eggs either directly on some part of the food plant or in a convenient place near the food supply, although there are exceptions. In some respects insect eggs are much like seeds—they are sometimes produced in fairly large numbers and vary in size and shape and often have sculptured surfaces; indeed, when viewed through the lens some are very beautiful objects.

If we examine the recently developed leaves of the apple in early spring, we would likely find the eggs of the codling moth, since this insect is a common pest of the apple. We usually think of eggs as being oval or spherical in shape, but surprisingly those of the codling moth are scale-like and white in color and about half the size of a pinhead. If we look on cabbage leaves at about the same time, we would likely find conical, pale yellow eggs, and if we viewed them through our lens we would see that they are ribbed (*Fig-*

ADVENTURE 39

We Stand Corrected that Eggs Are Not Always Egg-Shaped

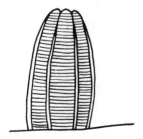

Figure 165
EGG OF CABBAGE BUTTERFLY

Figure 166
EGGS OF SQUASH BUG

Figure 167
EGG OF BLACK
SWALLOWTAIL BUTTERFLY

Figure 168
EGG OF FRUIT-FLY

ure 165). The eggs are those of the imported cabbage worm, a common and familiar insect we know more familiarly as the white butterfly we so often see flying about our gardens and fields in search of cabbage and related plants.

A little later, when squash leaves have developed, the squash bug, another common insect and rather injurious to squashes and other members of the squash family, appears and lays her eggs on the leaves. They are easy to find, for they are laid in clusters and are oval and pale yellow to brown (*Figure 166*).

After the carrot, parsnip, and celery have grown beyond the seedling stage, the leaves are frequently found with the pale yellowish eggs of the black swallowtail butterfly. The eggs are more or less spherical, as are all the eggs of the swallowtail tribe (*Figure 167*).

Not all insect eggs are laid in such exposed places; most of them are deposited in out-of-the-way places, as in the bark of trees and shrubs, in crevices and other hidden retreats, and within the tissues of plants, as in stems and leaves. The eggs of tree hoppers, leaf hoppers, and tree crickets are deposited in such places, and we do not ordinarily find them unless we actually are looking for them or if we inadvertently come upon them.

During the summer months when you are outdoors be sure to carry your lens with you and examine various plants, for you never know when or where you will find insect eggs. As you observe them through your lens, you will find that they may be smooth or variously sculptured, in some instances with small hexagonal areas; others may have ridges or show other forms of ornamentation. Though the ornamentation is often exquisitely beautiful, the patterns are probably of no particular use, being produced incidentally as impressions by the cells that secrete the eggshell.

Figure 169
EGG OF WATER SCORPION

Some eggs, strangely enough, are provided with appendages. This is true of certain species of fruit flies (*Figure 168*). The water scorpion, which lives in shallow water concealed in the mud or among dead leaves and twigs, lays eggs that have a crown of eight or more filaments (*Figure 169*). These eggs are laid in the tissues of decaying plants. The eggs of stinkbugs have a circle of spines around the upper edge (*Figure 170*). One member of this group lays white eggs in a double row on the leaves of cabbage and related plants that look like small barrels because of their two black bands and white spot (*Figure 171*). The insect that lays these eggs is known variously as the harlequin cabbage bug, or calico-back, the terrapin bug, or fire bug, and is shining black or deep blue profusely marked with red.

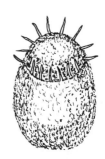

Figure 170
EGG OF STINKBUG

Figure 171
EGGS OF HARLEQUIN CABBAGE BUG

Figure 172
EGG OF WHEEL BUG

Figure 173
EGG OF POULTRY LOUSE

The assassin bugs include a number of different species, as the wheel bug, and are rather striking insects. They are all fairly large and some of them are gaily colored. Their eggs take various forms and may be cylindrical or elongate-oval (*Figure 172*). But it is not their shape that is of interest, rather the presence of a cap at one end which is pushed off in the hatching process and which is often decorated with raylike extensions. Of all the ornamental structures with which insect eggs may be furnished the most striking are undoubtedly those found on the eggs of the poultry louse. The eggs are white, elliptical, and are provided with white, glasslike spines (*Figure 173*). They are worth looking for and viewing through your lens if you are not averse to examining the feathers of chickens to which they are attached.

ADVENTURE 40

*We Play
Amateur Petrologists*

IN TERMS OF GEOLOGY a rock is a mineral found in large quantities in the earth or is a mixture, or aggregate, of minerals. The familiar granite is chiefly a mixture of three minerals, quartz, feldspar, and mica, whereas the less familiar sandstone is composed usually of a single mineral, quartz.

According to their origin, position in the

earth's crust, and location in respect to one another, rocks are divided into three main groups: igneous, made by the solidification of molten material; sedimentary, formed by the deposition of material by water, wind, and glacier; and metamorphic, produced by the action of heat and pressure on igneous and sedimentary rocks. Let us consider a common rock illustrative of each of these three groups.

We learned in Adventure 29 that certain substances will form crystals if dissolved in water and the water is allowed to evaporate. Similarly, if certain substances are heated, they will form crystals on cooling. Igneous rocks were formed in that way. So if we examine such a rock with our lens, we would expect to find crystals. View a fragment of granite through your lens and you will find that this is true. Some of the crystals you will probably recognize as quartz crystals. Present is another kind of crystal, which is monoclinic or needle-shaped, in form (*Figure 174*). This crystal is the mineral feldspar, which forms the whitish or pinkish portion of the rock. These two minerals are the essential constituents of granite, though there may be other minerals present, as hornblende, biotite, muscovite, and, to a lesser degree and only occasionally, epidote and tourmaline. Muscovite, more familiar to us as mica, is

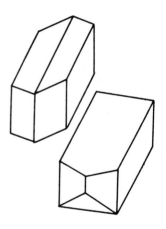

Figure 174
MONOCLINIC CRYSTALS OF FELDSPAR

181

extensively used in electrical insulations. It occurs as pearly scales that you can easily lift off with a knife. If black particles that are not easily separated into thin layers are present, they probably consist of the mineral hornblende.

Obviously sandstone is a rock formed from sand, but actually the word is used to describe any sedimentary rock whose particles are about the size of sand grains. When we view a fragment of sandstone through our lens, we find it composed of subangular to rounded grains we recognize as quartz. We may also observe that there are small spaces or pores between the grains,* although there are some sandstones without such pores. Some sandstones are composed entirely of grains held together by the compactness the rock, but in others the grains are held together by a cementing material that then fills all the pores. Essentially a sandstone consists of quartz grains, but frequently other minerals may be present, such as feldspar, muscovite, and calcite. I said at the beginning of this paragraph that in a sandstone the particles are about the size of sand grains. If the particles are smaller, less than one five hundredth of an inch, the sandstone grades into

---

* In general there is a considerable amount of space between the grains of sand so that a sandstone will absorb large amounts of water—up to 25% of its bulk.

shale; when they are larger than that of a pea, it grades into conglomerate. If a sandstone has been subjected to heat and pressure, it is then known as quartzite, a metamorphic rock. Frequently one grades into another. Quartzite may be distinguished from sandstone by the almost complete lack of pore spaces, its greater hardness, and by its crystalline structure. It may be further distinguished by the fact that a sandstone, in breaking, separates between the grains of sand, while a quartzite breaks through the grains.

In Adventure 35 we said that the mineral calcite is removed from water by various animals that use it in building shells or other structures in which to live. When the animals die the shells sink to the bottom, where they are pulverized and accumulate in large deposits of mudlike consistency which eventually are compressed to form a sedimentary rock. We know this rock as limestone. Through the lens a fragment of limestone appears much like sandstone. Pure limestone is white, but it may be variously colored by impurities. As in sandstone, other minerals may also be present. As you will recall that we can determine the identity of calcite by adding a drop of hydrochloric acid to it. Since limestone is calcite, we can apply the same test to a rock we suspect to be limestone.

If limestone has been subjected to heat and

pressure, it is then known as marble, also a metamorphic rock. Marble is a broad term. It is preferably used for any limestone that will take a polish and can be used commercially, whether it is sedimentary or metamorphic, but I am using it in connection with metamorphic limestone. Similarly, as in the case of quartzite, which is crystalline sandstone, marble is also crystalline, indeed, it has more crystalline structure than most metamorphic rocks. Pure marble is white but may be variously colored red, pink, green, and black by the presence of other minerals.

ADVENTURE 41

We Marvel at Nature's Ingenuity

WE KNOW THAT INSECTS are useful agents in the pollination of flowers—bees, for instance, are indispensable in the orchard—but few of us are aware of the intimate relationships that have been established between many flowers and their insect visitors. Many flowers have become structurally modified in such a way that the insects visiting them for their nectar cannot leave without carrying a number of pollen grains with them. The fantastic forms of orchids are really elaborate traps designed toward this end. So, too, are the flowers of the common milkweed.

Let us examine one of the latter. The milkweed is common everywhere—along the way-

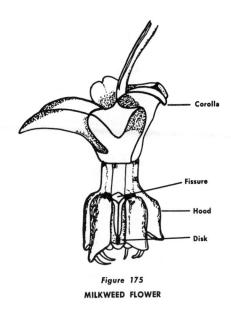

Corolla

Fissure

Hood

Disk

Figure 175
MILKWEED FLOWER

side, in fields and meadows, in waste places, along the woodland border—and its large, pendulous, cloyingly sweet flower clusters are conspicuous on the summer landscape. We need our lens and a needle. When we view one of the flowers we first observe the five hoods or nectar horns filled with nectar, located in front of each anther (*Figure 175*). We next look carefully between these hoods and find the white-bordered, V-shaped opening, or fissure, of a long pocket or slit, at the upper end of which is a black dot, or notched disk. We slip a needle into the pocket or fissure and extend it upward until it touches the black dot or disk, and if we then apply a slight pressure out pops a pair of yellow saddlebags, each attached to the disk. These yellow saddlebags are the pollen masses, or pollinia (*Figure 176*).

When a honeybee or other insect visits the milkweed and crawls over the flowers to get the nectar, its legs slip in between the hoods, and as a leg is drawn up, a claw, hair, or spine invariably catches in the V-shaped fissure and is guided along the slit to the notched disk. The disk clings to the claw, hair, or spine, and when the insect leaves it carries away with it the two attached pollen masses. You can see this for yourself if you station yourself by a milkweed plant and observe the behavior of an insect visitor through a reading glass when it alights on the flower cluster. I should add that when first removed from their enclosing pockets or anthers the two pollen masses lie in the same plane, but in a few seconds they twist on their stalks and come face to face in such a way that one of them can easily be introduced into the stigmatic chamber of a new flower visited by the insect.

Another common flower, also modified to ensure pollination by insect visitors and one we can easily examine, is the iris, or blue flag.

Figure 176
POLLINIA OF MILKWEED

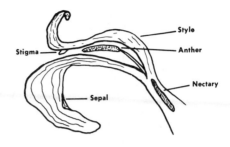

Figure 177
SECTION OF IRIS FLOWER

The iris is one of the more familiar spring flowers of swamps and marshes, and related members of the group are extensively cultivated in gardens. The blue flag, with its large showy blossoms, seems especially designed for bees, since blue is their favorite color, but other insects also visit it. Each of the three drooping sepals forms the floor of an arched passageway that leads to the nectary, the roof being formed by three straplike divisions of the style (the middle portion of the pistil). Over the entrance to the passageway and pointing outward is a movable lip, the stigma (*Figure 177*). In back of the stigma and beneath the roof is the stamen with its anther. When a bee visits the blossom, carrying pollen from another flower, it alights on the tip of the sepal, and then as it presses forward it hits and bends down the stigma, which scrapes the pollen from the back of the bee and then springs back into place. As the bee continues on its way toward the nectary, its hairy back rubs against the overhanging anther and becomes powdered with pollen grains. When it backs out of the passageway, after getting its fill of nectar, it again encounters the stigma, but this side of the stigma cannot receive pollen and so immediate close pollination is averted. Just how all this is accomplished may easily be observed through the reading glass by waiting for a bee to enter a blossom and then watching its actions.

The milkweed and iris are but two examples of structural modifications for insect pollination. There are countless others. The sage, nasturtium, and larkspur of our gardens come to mind. The butter-and-eggs, with its delightful two-lipped, spurred yellow and orange flowers and so common from July to October along roadsides and in waste places, and the jewelweed, blooming by the brookside, its bright flowers hanging like jewels from a lady's ears, also come to mind. Why not examine these and others, too, with your lens and discover, if you can, the various and often ingenious mechanisms that plants have developed to compel their insect visitors to carry their pollen to other flowers and thus ensure their survival as species.

HAVE YOU EVER NOTICED small flies about the fruit bowl or fruit basket especially in summer? Have you ever wondered what they were doing there? The larvae feed on ripe or over-ripe bananas and other fruit, and the flies we see about the fruit are either females preparing to lay their eggs in the fruit or newly developed adults recently emerged from their pupal state. The larvae also feed on vinegar, stale beer, and the like, hence the insects are variously called fruit flies, sour flies, vinegar flies, and pomace flies. They are, however, best known as fruit flies.

These flies are insects of distinction. Some years ago Thomas Hunt Morgan used them in studying heredity and sex, and because they lend themselves so readily to investigative work on such studies, they have been extensively used since then on both simple and complex cases of Mendelian inheritance and the relations between body characteristics and genes. There are several reasons why they are ideal experimental animals. One is that they reproduce quickly. The average duration of the egg period at ordinary room temperature is about two days; of the larval period about six days; and of the pupal period about five days. Another is that a bit of banana in a bottle is about all that is necessary to breed the insects.

We are not interested at present in inheri-

*We Breed
Some Flies*

tance or inherited characters, but in breeding a few generations. To do so, we need first of all a few flies, and the best time to get them is in the summertime. We can place some fruit in a dish and trust to luck that the flies will appear, or we can dip a piece of ripe banana in a suspension of yeast (which can easily be prepared by dissolving a quarter of a yeast cake in some water) and inserting the piece of banana along with a strip of paper toweling into a clean bottle. We can put the bottle aside or, better still, we can take it to our neighborhood fruit store and ask the owner if we can leave it there overnight. When we return to the store the following morning, there will be some flies in the bottle. We plug the bottle with some cotton wrapped in cheesecloth, take it home, and set it aside. We call this our culture bottle. Within two weeks we should have an ample supply of flies.

To breed the flies, we select a male and a female from our culture bottle and place them in another bottle, similar to the first, which we have meanwhile prepared. As the flies are small and active it will be almost impossible to transfer them unless we first render them unconscious. To do this, we must have an etherizer. We get a bottle having a mouth the same size as the mouth of the culture bottle. We insert a nail one inch long into a cork stopper that fits neatly into the mouth of the bottle and cover the nail with several layers of cotton, tying the cotton to the nail with thread or string. We then put a few drops of ether on the cotton, taking care not to use it near an open flame, since ether is highly inflammable.

We are now ready to transfer the flies from the culture bottle to the etherizer. We tap the culture bottle on the table so that the flies will drop to the bottom, quickly remove the cotton plug, and place the mouth of the etherizer closely against the mouth of the culture bottle. We next invert the two bottles and again tap the culture bottle so the flies will drop into the etherizer. To hasten the flies into the latter, we place an electric light near the etherizer because the flies are heliotropic and are attracted to light. When the flies have moved into the etherizer, we quickly separate the two bottles, replacing the cotton plug in the culture bottle and stopping the etherizer with the cork stopper containing the nail and cotton soaked with ether. The flies will be anesthetized in a few seconds.

When the flies are completely unconscious, we remove the stopper and spill them out on a piece of white paper. Since the flies will remain unconscious only a few minutes, we have to examine them quickly for our male and female. Frequently this may take a little

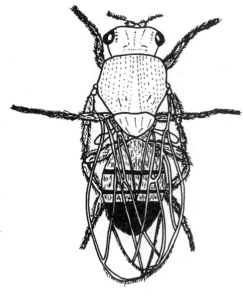

Figure 178
MALE FRUIT-FLY

longer than we anticipate, and the flies may
begin to show signs of recovering consciousness before we have been able to obtain our
mating pair. To guard against this, we have
on hand a shallow dish with a piece of blotting paper attached to it with a piece of adhe-
sive tape. If the flies show signs of recovering
consciousness, we add a drop or two of ether
to the paper and invert the dish over the flies
for a few seconds. We may have to repeat this
operation several times or until we have ob-

tained our male and female. As the flies are fragile it is advisable to handle them or to transfer them with a camel's-hair brush.

We need our lens in order to distinguish the male and female. How can we tell them apart? First of all, the male is a trifle smaller than the female and has a bluntly rounded abdomen with a wide band of dark pigment (*Figure 178*). The female's abdomen is elongated, with narrower pigment bands. Secondly, the male has five abdominal segments, the female seven. And thirdly, the female has an ovipositor or egg-laying apparatus, while the male has "sex combs" on the end of the tarsal joint of the front legs (*Figure 179*). These "sex combs" are black bristles and may be for the purpose of appearing more attractive to the females when he performs his courtship dance. The male, however, can be deprived of them without apparently lessening his chances with normal males for the favor of some female. Perhaps, as someone once said, they are used for cleaning his antennae, but then how does the female clean hers?

When we have separated a male and a female from the others, we place them in a second prepared culture bottle and await results. We can raise a third generation from their offspring and continue this breeding indefinitely.

Figure 179
SEX COMB OF MALE FRUIT-FLY

*We Explore
the Subject
of Variation*

Figure 180
AKENE OF DANDELION

THE DANDELION is such a common flower and so familiar to us that there seems to be little more we can say about it that we don't already know. In the spring the yellow flower heads appear in the fields and on our lawns and are shortly followed by the white heads that contain hundreds of seeds each provided with a little parachute tuft of fine silky hairs. If we look at one of these seeds through our lens, we will find it to be somewhat spindle-shaped, with four to five rough ribs and one end prolonged into a very slender beak that bears the fine silky hairs we just mentioned. (*Figure 180*). These hairs, as we all know, catch in the wind, which carries the seed about until it is finally deposited on the ground. But what about the other end? Here, too, we find hairs, but these are stiff. What purpose do they serve? They help the seed to cling to the ground when it lands and thus keep it in place until it can germinate and send down roots for anchorage.

The seed of the dandelion is not actually a seed in the botanical sense, but a fruit—a one-seeded fruit called an akene. The akenes are a very common type of fruit, although we may not think so because most of us see so few of them, and are produced by a large number of different kinds of flowers. Since these flowers differ from one another, we might suspect that the akenes differ also, and

Figure 181
AKENE OF MEADOW BUTTERCUP

Figure 182
AKENE OF EARLY BUTTERCUP

Figure 183
AKENE OF FIELD SORREL

this is so. Basically they are much alike, but variations occur, although sometimes they are minor, so that we can often tell by looking at an akene which plant produced it. The akene of the meadow buttercup, for instance, is compressed, with a short beak, and is pictured in *Figure 181*. The akene of the early buttercup, which is a woodland or hillside species, has an awl-like beak (*Figure 182*).

The field, or sheep, sorrel is a troublesome weed, with long, arrowhead leaves and inconspicuous green flowers. The flowers later turn brown red and eventually develop into akenes that are without a beak (*Figure 183*). The akene of the related buckwheat is somewhat similar in form but granular and marked with lines (*Figure 184*). Another relative, the

Figure 184
AKENE OF BUCKWHEAT

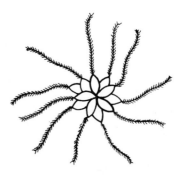

Figure 187
AKENE OF CLEMATIS

Figure 185
AKENE OF SMARTWEED

Figure 186
AKENE OF CINQUEFOIL

smartweed, or water pepper, has an akene that is three-angled and broadly oblong or ovoid (*Figure 185*). *Figure 186* shows an akene of the common cinquefoil, whose yellow flowers decorate meadow and pasture in early spring and are sometimes incorrectly called the wild strawberry. The little seeds of the strawberry, incidentally, are akenes. In some instances the akenes are furnished with plumose appendages (*Figure 187*) as in the clematis, or virgin's-bower, a beautiful trailing vine commonly found draped over bushes in copses and by moist roadsides. When viewed through the lens they appear like many tiny, twisted tails.

Figure 188
AKENE OF CHICORY

Figure 189
AKENE OF SUNFLOWER

Figure 190
AKENE OF SNEEZEWEED

Speaking of appendages, the akenes of various composites are furnished with various appendages in the form of scales, hooks, barbs, and chaff. The appendage, no matter what its form, is called a pappus. In the chicory it is a shallow cup (*Figure 188*), in the sunflower it consists of two deciduous scales (*Figure 189*), in the sneezeweed of five scales (*Figure 190*), in the sow thistle of delicate, downy hairs (*Figure 191*), and in the dandelion it is made up of a number of silky hairs that are attached to the long, tapering beak of the akene (*Figure 180*) After you have examined these few akenes, you should be able to find many more.

Figure 191
AKENE OF SOW THISTLE

ADVENTURE 44

We Get to Know the Barnacle

THOSE OF US WHO LIVE near the coast can find many things of interest along the sea beach, not the least of which are the barnacles. Barnacles are shrimplike animals that live within a calcareous shell. They are familiar objects along the rocky shore. Because of their shell they were at one time believed to be mollusks, but since they have jointed appendages they are now placed among the arthropods. The appendages are fringed like feathers and are drawn into or protruded from the shell at will. When the animal is covered with water the appendages are extended out of the shell and sweep through the water like a casting net, capturing small swimming creatures and organic fragments that serve as food.

The life history of the barnacle is most interesting. The young barnacle, which hatches from the egg, is free-swimming and in no way resembles the adult. After swimming about for a while it undergoes changes and then settles on some solid object, such as a rock, wharf pile, drifting timber, the bottom of a ship, and even on a whale, fastening itself, head foremost, by means of a cementlike secretion. (If you think barnacles are not securely attached just try to pry one off). After it has found a permanent location it undergoes further changes until it has attained its adult form.

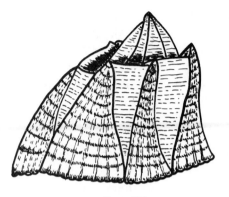

Figure 192
BARNACLE

There are several different kinds of barnacles, but the one familiar to most of us is
the rock barnacle, which we find attached to
rocks along the shore. Sometimes the rocks
are so thickly covered with the barnacles that
they appear white from a distance. If we look
at the shell through our lens, we find it composed of a number of thick calcareous plates
that fit together in a tentlike form (*Figure
192*). These plates, which are usually six in
number, are rigidly attached to each other
and to a fold of skin surrounding the body of
the animal, but there are two pairs of hinged
valves at the top which may open and close
like double doors. It is said that if you tap
a rock encrusted with barnacles and hold

your ear near you can hear the closing of many doors.

If you visit the seashore when the rocks are covered with water and if the barnacles are unmolested, you will see thousands of tiny fringed feet waving to and fro. They are extended out through the open doors and serve as a sort of casting net. Their movements are perfectly regular and rapid and may beat back and forth as many as a hundred times a minute. As someone once remarked, a barnacle is a little shrimplike animal standing on its head within a limestone house and kicking its food into its mouth with its feet.

ADVENTURE 45

We Seek the Liverwort

IF YOU LOOK along the mossy bank of a brook or stream or among the mosses in damp woods, you should find flat, ribbonlike plants growing close to the ground. They are papery thin and may be either long and slender or repeatedly lobed and forked. In a way they resemble the lichens except that they are distinctly green in color. Called liverworts,* they are very simple plants without stem or leaves. Of no economic importance, they are of interest, however, because

---

* The name "liverwort" is derived from the somewhat liver-shaped thallus and the belief at one time that they could cure diseases of the liver.

they represent the transition stage from a water living habit to a land living habit, in other words, they bridge the gap between the algae, which are fundamentally aquatic, and the higher flowering land plants.

There are some four thousand species of liverworts, but one of the most common and the one you are most apt to find is Marchantia, a name derived from a French botanist who lived about three hundred years ago. It has a peculiar dull-green color with a broad, ribbon-shaped thallus, which is simply a plant without true roots, stems or leaves, and generally forked once or twice. The upper surface is divided into angular areas in the center of which we can distinguish an air pore. If you will examine the lower surface with your lens, you will find numerous hairs, called rhizoids, that anchor it to the ground and that serve to some extent the same purpose as the roots of higher plants.

Note if umbrella-like structures extend into the air from the surface of the thallus. These upright growths are the reproductive organs. The umbrella part may be either flat, shield-shaped, radially lobed, or it may be a disk with deep, fingerlike lobes that usually curve downward. The former is the male organ, or antheridial disk (*Figure 193*), the latter the female, or archegonial disk (*Figure 194*), and you will not find them on

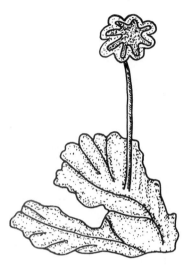

Figure 193
ANTHEREDIAL DISK OF MARCHANTIA

Figure 194
ARCHEGONIAL DISK OF MARCHANTIA

the same plant. Sperms are produced in the male organ and eggs in the female, and since these organs occur on separate plants, it is necessary for the sperms to swim to the eggs so that the latter may be fertilized. This explains why liverworts always grow in wet or damp places. At first there seems to be a considerable element of chance involved in this method of reproduction, for the question arises, how do the sperms locate the eggs? The probability of a sperm's locating an egg would appear to be one in a million, if the odds are not even greater. Actually the

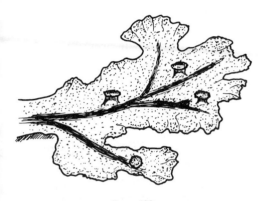

Figure 195

GEMMAE CUPS OF MARCHANTIA

Figure 196

GEMMA OF MARCHANTIA

sperms have no difficulty finding the eggs because the female organ discharges substances that help to orient the sperms in the right direction. The phenomenon is called positive chemotaxis.

Instead of the umbrella-like structures you may find little cup-shaped or saucer-shaped structures with toothed margins on the upper surface of the thallus (*Figure 195*). These structures produce green disks called gemmae, or brood bodies (*Figure 196*). When washed out or blown to some distant place they grow into new plants.

THE DICTIONARY TELLS US that a trap is a device that shuts suddenly with a springlike action for taking game and other animals. Man has devised many ingenious traps, but I doubt if he has improved upon those designed by nature or will ever do so. I am thinking specifically of the traps developed by certain plants for catching insects. Best known are the Venus-flytrap, the sundew, and the pitcher plant. Perhaps you are familiar with them.

The Bladderwort (*Figure 197*) is perhaps not quite so generally known, but it has designed a trap that, I think, is more ingenious than those developed by the plants mentioned above. It is a plant of ponds and sluggish streams, delicate and vinelike in appearance, and floats beneath the surface among the stems of water lilies and pondweeds. Without roots it has instead twiglike rhizoids that function as roots. The stem is slender and bears finely branched leaves arranged alternately but divided so closely to the base that each leaf appears to be two leaves growing opposite one another. The leaves are furnished with small bladders that at one time were believed to function entirely as floats but which also serve as traps for capturing small aquatic creatures. They deserve our attention, so let us examine them.

To do so, we need to lift the plant out of

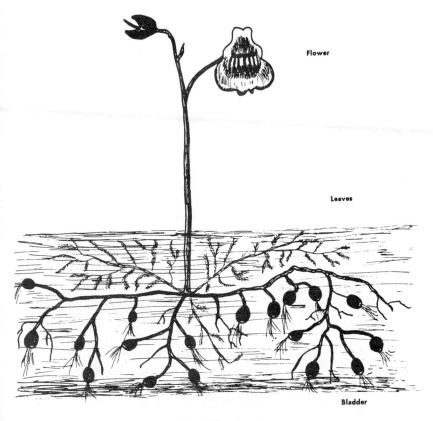

Figure 197
BLADDERWORT

the water, and when we look at one of them
through our lens we find it a slightly compressed sac with a slit-shaped opening (*Figure 198*). The opening is guarded by a valve,

or trap door, that opens only inward, and the rim of the opening is armed with teeth and bristling hairs. Within the bladder are more hairs.

How does the trap door operate? When an unwary water animal swims into the opening, its movements stimulate the valve to open. As the sides of the bladder are ordinarily dented inward, the moment the valve opens water flows into the bladder and presses on the walls, which are then pushed outward. This inward flow of water creates a suction that results in the flowing of more water into the bladder. You have read how a sinking ship creates a suction and pulls down with it anything within the area of the suction, and why sailors, when they abandon a ship, are in a hurry to get away from it. The trap of the bladderwort functions in a similar manner. As the water flows into the trap, the animal responsible for starting the flow is carried into the trap, as well as others that may be caught in the suction. Once within the bladder there is no escape, because the valve is strongly elastic and snaps shut behind them. What is the fate of the imprisoned animals? They are digested by secretions produced by the walls of the bladder, and the digested material is then absorbed by the plant as food.

You can observe the operation of the traps if you take home a bladderwort and place it

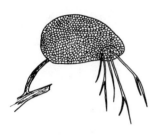

Figure 198
BLADDER OF BLADDERWORT

in an aquarium filled with clear water and well supplied with water fleas and other small aquatic creatures. For best results take a plant whose bladders are empty. The water fleas and other animals can be obtained from the same pond or stream where you found the plant by merely scooping out a pan full of water and transferring it to a bottle. Or you can submerge a large, widemouth bottle and allow the water to run into it. When observing the traps function it is advisable to use a reading glass rather than a small hand lens or pocket magnifier, since you probably can't get close enough with the latter to see what takes place.

I should add, as a final word, that the bladders, which at one time were believed to act as floats, actually function as such at the time of the flowering season. At that time they become filled with air and serve as pontoons to buoy up the plant so that the yellow flowers may be kept out of the water where insects can visit and pollinate them (*Figure 197*).

AT ONE TIME herbs were used extensively in cooking to improve the taste and flavor of various foods, and in recent years they have again become very popular. Almost everyone

Figure 199
SPEARMINT LEAF WITH OIL GLANDS

Figure 200
AKENE OF WILD CARROT

who has a garden has a few herbs growing in it. They may be used throughout the growing season or harvested in the fall, dried, and placed in jars. Many roadside stands at this time of the year have attractive displays, and many stores carry them throughout the year.

The substances used in adding taste and flavor to foods, drinks, and confections are basically aromatic oils secreted by glands or similar structures in the stems, leaves, and fruits of certain plants. For instance, if we examined a spearmint leaf with our hand lens, we would find the surface dotted with numerous small glands (*Figure 199*). The spearmint is a member of the mint family, a group of plants that are essentially aromatic and include peppermint, thyme, and marjoram, savory and sage. Examine the leaves of any of these plants and you will find them dotted with glands.

The aromatic oils that give such plants as dill and fennel, caraway and coriander their characteristic odors and tastes are produced not by glands in the leaves but by oil tubes located in the seeds or, more strictly speaking, in the fruits, which are akenes. All these plants are members of the parsley family, to which the wild carrot also belongs. As most of us may not have access to dill or fennel, caraway or coriander, we shall examine the akene of the wild carrot, which is common everywhere. Viewing it through our lens, we observe that it looks like a miniature green barrel beset with spines (*Figure 200*), which may lead some of you to think of the porcupine. We note also longitudinal ribs. Between these ribs are oil tubes, or vittae. Cut the akene transversely with a razor blade and you can see the ends of the tubes (*Figure 201*). Unlike other members of the family, the akene of the wild carrot produces oil that is not particularly pleasing to our taste. I might add that if you examine the akenes after they have matured you will find them brown instead of green.

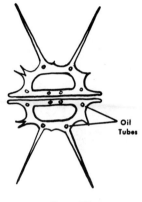

Figure 201
TRANSVERSE SECTION OF AKENE OF WILD CARROT

TAKE A SLICE OF BREAD, soak it in water, place it in a saucer, set the saucer aside for an hour or so, then cover the bread with a tumbler, and place it in a warm, dark place. Within two or three days you should find a cottony or cobwebby-like growth on the bread.

Examine this growth with your lens and you will find it composed of long threads passing in and out among each other forming a web (*Figure 202*). This tangled mass of threads is called a mycelium and forms the vegetative part of a fungus plant familiar to us as bread mold. The threads, which collectively compose the mycelium, are called

ADVENTURE 48

We Assume the Role of Farmers

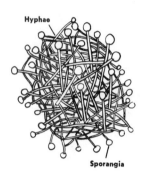

Figure 202
MYCELIUM OF BREAD MOLD

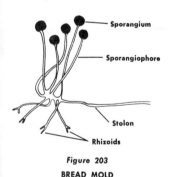

Figure 203
BREAD MOLD

hyphae. Some of the hyphae penetrate the bread and serve as absorptive structures called rhizoids; others grow over the surface of the bread and are called stolons. If you examine the latter carefully, you should see other hyphae extending upward from them and bearing at the tips small, pearl-like globules (*Figure 202*). These aerial hyphae are known as sporangiophores, and the globules as sporangia. Within the sporangia, spores are formed. As the spores ripen, the sporangia turn black and the entire mold plant acquires a black appearance (*Figure 203*). When the spores have fully matured the walls of the sporangia rupture, the spores are released and carried about by air currents. Upon encountering favorable conditions for growth a spore germinates, producing a hypha, which, by an extensive branching growth, forms a new mycelium and we have another mold plant.

On the same piece of bread may appear molds that are blue, green, or yellow in color, or if we should repeat the above procedure with a piece of cheese, a piece of orange rind, or some other food there should appear within a few days one of these colored molds. These molds are essentially like the bread mold except that the spores, instead of being borne within tiny globules, are borne in chains at the tip of certain hyphae. The

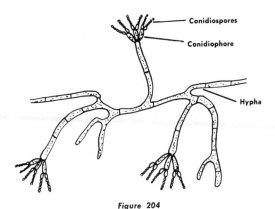

Figure 204
COMMON BLUE MOLD

spores are called conidiospores and the hyphae that bear them are called conidiophores
and resemble tiny brooms (*Figure 204*). The
conidiospores are produced in great numbers
and are very small and light in weight. When
mature they become detached and are carried
about by air currents, and when they find
favorable conditions quickly germinate and
develop into new mold plants. Since the
spores are variously colored, the characteristic color of the mold is due to the color of
their conidial masses.

Since our experience with molds may be
limited to those that appear on our foods,
leather goods, fabrics, tobacco, and other or-

ganic materials, we may get the erroneous impression that all molds are harmful. It is true that many of them are destructive agents in the spoilage of foods, while others are responsible for several diseases, yet some species are quite useful, as those that are agents in the decay of dead plant and animal bodies and thus help in the maintenance of soil fertility. Others are used in the manufacture of alcohol from rice starch and in the commercial production of various organic acids. The characteristic odors and flavors of certain well-known types of cheese are due to their metabolic activities in the butterfat and casein of milk. One species has received considerable publicity in recent years as the source of a bactericial drug, penicillin, which is used to destroy certain pathogenic organisms responsible for a number of human diseases.

ADVENTURE 49

We Are Intrigued by an Ingenious Mechanism

IN SPITE OF ITS NAME a starfish is not a fish. Perhaps "sea star" would be a better name, since it is shaped like a star and lives in the sea. To many of us starfish are animals in name only, but to most of us who live near the coast they are actually living creatures we find in tide pools and among the rocks along the seashore. They are rather odd animals

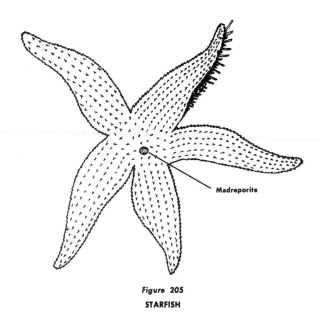

Figure 205
STARFISH

with a spiny skin and a body consisting of a central disk from which radiate a number of arms. In the common starfish there are five arms, but the number varies according to the species. Apart from their harmful tendencies of preying upon oysters, starfish are of no importance. Why, then, do we make them the subject of this Adventure?

Starfish have a peculiar way of moving around. Movement is effected by a number of structures called tube feet, which are operated by a sort of hydraulic-pressure mechanism. Viewed through a lens or reading glass, the manner in which these tube feet function is most interesting. So let us go to the seashore and look in the tide pools or among the rocks for them. The best time is when the tide is out, for they are usually found below the low-water mark. As we pick one up the first feature we notice is an orange disk on the upper surface and called the madreporite (*Figure 205*). Actually it is a sieve plate, and if we examine it with our lens we note that it is provided with minute openings. Water enters through these openings and passes down a tube called the stone canal, so-named because its wall is made rigid by calcareous rings. This canal opens into a circular tube that runs around the mouth, which we can locate by turning the animal over and looking at the lower surface. The circular tube, known as the ring canal, in turn connects with radial canals that run the length of the arms. There is a canal for each arm, so in a starfish with five arms there are five of these canals. The water upon flowing down the stone canal enters the ring canal and then flows along each of the radial canals. What happens to the water now? Again looking at the lower surface of the starfish and particularly at the lower surface of the arms, we observe a groove (ambulacral groove) that runs along the length of the arms. If we now place the fingers of one hand on one side of the groove and the fingers on the other hand on the other side and press gently, we can open the groove, and as we do so we find a number of odd-shaped structures that appear through a lens as cylinders ending in what seem like disks. These odd-shaped structures are hollow and thin-walled and are called tube feet. Each is connected by a short branch to the radial canal and further connects with a rounded muscular sac, the ampulla (*Figure 206*). The ampulla extends within the arm, and we cannot see it unless we dissect the animal.

And now to answer the question, what happens to the water when it flows along the radial canal? Since the tube feet are connected to the radial canal, the water enters the ampullae, and when the ampullae contract, through muscular action, the water is forced into the tube feet, which become distended, and the bottom of the foot, the sucker, becomes pressed against the substratum. But why doesn't the water flow back into the radial canal, you ask, when the ampullae are contracted? Simply because a valve prevents the water from doing so. To continue: After the tube feet have become distended, longitudinal muscles, with which they are provided, are brought into play,

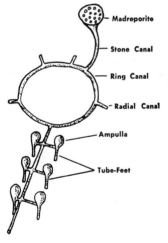

Figure 206

DIAGRAM OF WATER-VASCULAR SYSTEM

shortening the tube feet, forcing the water back into the ampullae, and drawing the animal forward. One tube foot, of course, is not particularly effective, but the combined efforts of hundreds of tube feet are capable of moving the animal.

If you are skeptical that the tube feet are able to exert enough force to move a starfish in this manner, try to open a live clam or oyster barehanded. You will find it almost impossible. But a starfish, which is not much larger then either of these animals, does it easily. The starfish mounts the clam or oyster in a humped-up position, attaches its tube feet to the two shells, and begins to pull. The clam or oyster reacts to the attack of the starfish by closing its two shells tightly. But the starfish continues to pull and by using its tube feet in relays is able to outlast the clam or oyster, whose muscles finally become fatigued and relax. When the shells gape the starfish turns the lower part of its stomach inside out, extends it through its mouth in between the two shells, and proceeds to digest the soft parts of the clam or oyster.

As you watch the movement of the tube feet through your reading glass, note the movable spines on either side of the ambulacral groove. These spines can be brought close together and thus protect the soft tube feet when the starfish is attacked.

IN SPRING, about the time apple blossoms begin to show a touch of pink, we sometimes find on cedar trees brown swellings from which extend numerous long, thin, bright orange tendrils, or horns, that twist about like petals of a flower (*Figure 207*). Known as cedar apples, they excite our interest by their curious appearance. Perhaps you have seen them and wondered what they were.

Actually they are galls, but, unlike those we have already discussed (see Adventure 37), are produced by a fungus plant. There is more to it than this, however, for these galls produce spores that are one of several kinds involved in a rather complex life history. The plant is known as the apple rust and is in reality a disease of the apple. Why it is called a rust we shall see presently.

The tendrils, or horns, which are small at first but which grow longer with every spring shower, produce a certain kind of spores called teliospores. These teliospores develop within the tendrils, or horns, into a second kind, known as basidiospores. When fully ripe the basidiospores are released and carried by the wind. If they fall on apple or crab-apple leaves and the conditions are favorable, they germinate quickly, penetrate the leaves, and produce a mycelium that branches throughout the leaf tissues. Their presence in the leaves may be detected by the appear-

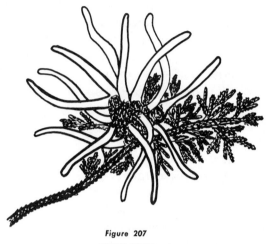

Figure 207
CEDAR APPLE

ance of yellow spots. The yellow spots resemble rust, whence the name, and if we examine them with our lens we find amber blisters. These blisters contain flask-shaped structures, pycnia (singular pycnium), which increase in size and exude a sticky substance. This exudation contains a third kind of spores called pycniospores.

The pycniospores are one of two sexes and a pycniospore of one sex must reach one of the other sex for fertilization to take place. This is effected by insects that are attracted to the exudation. After fertilization the pycnia change into black dots (*Figure 208*) surrounded by a reddish circle, and at the same time the fungus grows through the leaf, forming structures that appear through our lens as small cups with recurved and fringed or toothed margins (*Figure 209*). These cups, called aecia (singular aecium), produce still another kind of spores, called aeciospores. The spores mature in July and August and, like the basidiospores, are scattered by the wind. If they land on cedar leaves they germinate and produce by the following June small, greenish-brown swellings, or galls. The galls gradually increase in size until by autumn they have become chocolate brown and kidney-shaped, with small, circular depressions. They remain in this form until the following April, when, under the influence of spring showers, they begin to put forth the tendrils, or horns. After successive showers the horns grow longer and longer until the galls, covered with these horns, sometimes get to be the size of a small orange. Another crop of teliospores is now produced, thus completing the life cycle in something like two years. A point worth noting is that the rust cannot spread from cedar to cedar or from apple to apple, but must alternate between the two hosts.

Chief injury is to the apple, the rust causing premature defoliation, dwarfing, and

Figure 208
APPLE LEAF WITH PYCNIA

Figure 209
APPLE LEAF WITH AECIA

fruit of poor quality. Control methods, however, have reduced infection on orchard trees.
Most damage, today, is to crab apples planted
as ornamentals.

A CATALOGUE OF SELECTED DOVER BOOKS
IN ALL FIELDS OF INTEREST

A CATALOGUE OF SELECTED DOVER BOOKS
IN ALL FIELDS OF INTEREST

THE NOTEBOOKS OF LEONARDO DA VINCI, edited by J.P. Richter. Extracts from manuscripts reveal great genius; on painting, sculpture, anatomy, sciences, geography, etc. Both Italian and English. 186 ms. pages reproduced, plus 500 additional drawings, including studies for Last Supper, Sforza monument, etc. 860pp. 7⅞ x 10¾. USO 22572-0, 22573-9 Pa., Two vol. set $12.00

ART NOUVEAU DESIGNS IN COLOR, Alphonse Mucha, Maurice Verneuil, Georges Auriol. Full-color reproduction of Combinaisons ornementales (c. 1900) by Art Nouveau masters. Floral, animal, geometric, interlacings, swashes — borders, frames, spots — all incredibly beautiful. 60 plates, hundreds of designs. 9⅜ x 8¹/₁₆. 22885-1 Pa. $4.00

GRAPHIC WORKS OF ODILON REDON. All great fantastic lithographs, etchings, engravings, drawings, 209 in all. Monsters, Huysmans, still life work, etc. Introduction by Alfred Werner. 209pp. 9⅛ x 12¼. 21996-8 Pa. $5.00

EXOTIC FLORAL PATTERNS IN COLOR, E.-A. Seguy. Incredibly beautiful full-color pochoir work by great French designer of 20's. Complete Bouquets et frondaisons, Suggestions pour étoffes. Richness must be seen to be believed. 40 plates containing 120 patterns. 80pp. 9⅜ x 12¼. 23041-4 Pa. $6.00

SELECTED ETCHINGS OF JAMES A. McN. WHISTLER, James A. McN. Whistler. 149 outstanding etchings by the great American artist, including selections from the Thames set and two Venice sets, the complete French set, and many individual prints. Introduction and explanatory note on each print by Maria Naylor. 157pp. 9⅜ x 12¼. 23194-1 Pa. $5.00

VISUAL ILLUSIONS: THEIR CAUSES, CHARACTERISTICS, AND APPLICATIONS, Matthew Luckiesh. Thorough description, discussion; shape and size, color, motion; natural illusion. Uses in art and industry. 100 illustrations. 252pp. 21530-X Pa. $2.50

TEN BOOKS ON ARCHITECTURE, Vitruvius. The most important book ever written on architecture. Early Roman aesthetics, technology, classical orders, site selection, all other aspects. Stands behind everything since. Morgan translation. 331pp. 20645-9 Pa. $3.50

THE CODEX NUTTALL, A PICTURE MANUSCRIPT FROM ANCIENT MEXICO, as first edited by Zelia Nuttall. Only inexpensive edition, in full color, of a pre-Columbian Mexican (Mixtec) book. 88 color plates show kings, gods, heroes, temples, sacrifices. New explanatory, historical introduction by Arthur G. Miller. 96pp. 11⅜ x 8½. 23168-2 Pa. $7.50

CREATIVE LITHOGRAPHY AND HOW TO DO IT, Grant Arnold. Lithography as art form: working directly on stone, transfer of drawings, lithotint, mezzotint, color printing; also metal plates. Detailed, thorough. 27 illustrations. 214pp.
21208-4 Pa. $3.00

DESIGN MOTIFS OF ANCIENT MEXICO, Jorge Enciso. Vigorous, powerful ceramic stamp impressions — Maya, Aztec, Toltec, Olmec. Serpents, gods, priests, dancers, etc. 153pp. 6⅛ x 9¼.
20084-1 Pa. $2.50

AMERICAN INDIAN DESIGN AND DECORATION, Leroy Appleton. Full text, plus more than 700 precise drawings of Inca, Maya, Aztec, Pueblo, Plains, NW Coast basketry, sculpture, painting, pottery, sand paintings, metal, etc. 4 plates in color. 279pp. 8⅜ x 11¼.
22704-9 Pa. $4.50

CHINESE LATTICE DESIGNS, Daniel S. Dye. Incredibly beautiful geometric designs: circles, voluted, simple dissections, etc. Inexhaustible source of ideas, motifs. 1239 illustrations. 469pp. 6⅛ x 9¼.
23096-1 Pa. $5.00

JAPANESE DESIGN MOTIFS, Matsuya Co. Mon, or heraldic designs. Over 4000 typical, beautiful designs: birds, animals, flowers, swords, fans, geometric; all beautifully stylized. 213pp. 11⅜ x 8¼.
22874-6 Pa. $4.95

PERSPECTIVE, Jan Vredeman de Vries. 73 perspective plates from 1604 edition; buildings, townscapes, stairways, fantastic scenes. Remarkable for beauty, surrealistic atmosphere; real eye-catchers. Introduction by Adolf Placzek. 74pp. 11⅜ x 8¼.
20186-4 Pa. $2.75

EARLY AMERICAN DESIGN MOTIFS, Suzanne E. Chapman. 497 motifs, designs, from painting on wood, ceramics, appliqué, glassware, samplers, metal work, etc. Florals, landscapes, birds and animals, geometrics, letters, etc. Inexhaustible. Enlarged edition. 138pp. 8⅜ x 11¼.
22985-8 Pa. $3.50
23084-8 Clothbd. $7.95

VICTORIAN STENCILS FOR DESIGN AND DECORATION, edited by E.V. Gillon, Jr. 113 wonderful ornate Victorian pieces from German sources; florals, geometrics; borders, corner pieces; bird motifs, etc. 64pp. 9⅜ x 12¼.
21995-X Pa. $2.50

ART NOUVEAU: AN ANTHOLOGY OF DESIGN AND ILLUSTRATION FROM THE STUDIO, edited by E.V. Gillon, Jr. Graphic arts: book jackets, posters, engravings, illustrations, decorations; Crane, Beardsley, Bradley and many others. Inexhaustible. 92pp. 8⅛ x 11.
22388-4 Pa. $2.50

ORIGINAL ART DECO DESIGNS, William Rowe. First-rate, highly imaginative modern Art Deco frames, borders, compositions, alphabets, florals, insectals, Wurlitzer-types, etc. Much finest modern Art Deco. 80 plates, 8 in color. 8⅜ x 11¼.
22567-4 Pa. $3.00

HANDBOOK OF DESIGNS AND DEVICES, Clarence P. Hornung. Over 1800 basic geometric designs based on circle, triangle, square, scroll, cross, etc. Largest such collection in existence. 261pp.
20125-2 Pa. $2.50

150 MASTERPIECES OF DRAWING, edited by Anthony Toney. 150 plates, early 15th century to end of 18th century; Rembrandt, Michelangelo, Dürer, Fragonard, Watteau, Wouwerman, many others. 150pp. 8⅜ x 11¼.   21032-4 Pa. $3.50

THE GOLDEN AGE OF THE POSTER, Hayward and Blanche Cirker. 70 extraordinary posters in full colors, from Maîtres de l'Affiche, Mucha, Lautrec, Bradley, Cheret, Beardsley, many others. 9⅜ x 12¼.   22753-7 Pa. $4.95
21718-3 Clothbd. $7.95

SIMPLICISSIMUS, selection, translations and text by Stanley Appelbaum. 180 satirical drawings, 16 in full color, from the famous German weekly magazine in the years 1896 to 1926. 24 artists included: Grosz, Kley, Pascin, Kubin, Kollwitz, plus Heine, Thöny, Bruno Paul, others. 172pp. 8½ x 12¼.   23098-8 Pa. $5.00
23099-6 Clothbd. $10.00

THE EARLY WORK OF AUBREY BEARDSLEY, Aubrey Beardsley. 157 plates, 2 in color: Manon Lescaut, Madame Bovary, Morte d'Arthur, Salome, other. Introduction by H. Marillier. 175pp. 8½ x 11.   21816-3 Pa. $3.50

THE LATER WORK OF AUBREY BEARDSLEY, Aubrey Beardsley. Exotic masterpieces of full maturity: Venus and Tannhäuser, Lysistrata, Rape of the Lock, Volpone, Savoy material, etc. 174 plates, 2 in color. 176pp. 8½ x 11.   21817-1 Pa. $3.75

DRAWINGS OF WILLIAM BLAKE, William Blake. 92 plates from Book of Job, Divine Comedy, Paradise Lost, visionary heads, mythological figures, Laocoön, etc. Selection, introduction, commentary by Sir Geoffrey Keynes. 178pp. 8½ x 11.   22303-5 Pa. $3.50

LONDON: A PILGRIMAGE, Gustave Doré, Blanchard Jerrold. Squalor, riches, misery, beauty of mid-Victorian metropolis; 55 wonderful plates, 125 other illustrations, full social, cultural text by Jerrold. 191pp. of text. 8⅛ x 11.   22306-X Pa. $5.00

THE COMPLETE WOODCUTS OF ALBRECHT DÜRER, edited by Dr. W. Kurth. 346 in all: Old Testament, St. Jerome, Passion, Life of Virgin, Apocalypse, many others. Introduction by Campbell Dodgson. 285pp. 8½ x 12¼.   21097-9 Pa. $6.00

THE DISASTERS OF WAR, Francisco Goya. 83 etchings record horrors of Napoleonic wars in Spain and war in general. Reprint of 1st edition, plus 3 additional plates. Introduction by Philip Hofer. 97pp. 9⅜ x 8¼.   21872-4 Pa. $2.50

ENGRAVINGS OF HOGARTH, William Hogarth. 101 of Hogarth's greatest works: Rake's Progress, Harlot's Progress, Illustrations for Hudibras, Midnight Modern Conversation, Before and After, Beer Street and Gin Lane, many more. Full commentary. 256pp. 11 x 14.   22479-1 Pa. $6.00
23023-6 Clothbd. $13.50

PRIMITIVE ART, Franz Boas. Great anthropologist on ceramics, textiles, wood, stone, metal, etc.; patterns, technology, symbols, styles. All areas, but fullest on Northwest Coast Indians. 350 illustrations. 378pp.   20025-6 Pa. $3.50

CONSTRUCTION OF AMERICAN FURNITURE TREASURES, Lester Margon. 344 detail drawings, complete text on constructing exact reproductions of 38 early American masterpieces: Hepplewhite sideboard, Duncan Phyfe drop-leaf table, mantel clock, gate-leg dining table, Pa. German cupboard, more. 38 plates. 54 photographs. 168pp. 8⅜ x 11¼. 23056-2 Pa. $4.00

JEWELRY MAKING AND DESIGN, Augustus F. Rose, Antonio Cirino. Professional secrets revealed in thorough, practical guide: tools, materials, processes; rings, brooches, chains, cast pieces, enamelling, setting stones, etc. Do not confuse with skimpy introductions: beginner can use, professional can learn from it. Over 200 illustrations. 306pp. 21750-7 Pa. $3.00

METALWORK AND ENAMELLING, Herbert Maryon. Generally coneeded best all-around book. Countless trade secrets: materials, tools, soldering, filigree, setting, inlay, niello, repoussé, casting, polishing, etc. For beginner or expert. Author was foremost British expert. 330 illustrations. 335pp. 22702-2 Pa. $3.50

WEAVING WITH FOOT-POWER LOOMS, Edward F. Worst. Setting up a loom, beginning to weave, constructing equipment, using dyes, more, plus over 285 drafts of traditional patterns including Colonial and Swedish weaves. More than 200 other figures. For beginning and advanced. 275pp. 8¾ x 6⅜. 23064-3 Pa. $4.00

WEAVING A NAVAJO BLANKET, Gladys A. Reichard. Foremost anthropologist studied under Navajo women, reveals every step in process from wool, dyeing, spinning, setting up loom, designing, weaving. Much history, symbolism. With this book you could make one yourself. 97 illustrations. 222pp. 22992-0 Pa. $3.00

NATURAL DYES AND HOME DYEING, Rita J. Adrosko. Use natural ingredients: bark, flowers, leaves, lichens, insects etc. Over 135 specific recipes from historical sources for cotton, wool, other fabrics. Genuine premodern handicrafts. 12 illustrations. 160pp. 22688-3 Pa. $2.00

THE HAND DECORATION OF FABRICS, Francis J. Kafka. Outstanding, profusely illustrated guide to stenciling, batik, block printing, tie dyeing, freehand painting, silk screen printing, and novelty decoration. 356 illustrations. 198pp. 6 x 9. 21401-X Pa. $3.00

THOMAS NAST: CARTOONS AND ILLUSTRATIONS, with text by Thomas Nast St. Hill. Father of American political cartooning. Cartoons that destroyed Tweed Ring; inflation, free love, church and state; original Republican elephant and Democratic donkey; Santa Claus; more. 117 illustrations. 146pp. 9 x 12. 22983-1 Pa. $4.00
23067-8 Clothbd. $8.50

FREDERIC REMINGTON: 173 DRAWINGS AND ILLUSTRATIONS. Most famous of the Western artists, most responsible for our myths about the American West in its untamed days. Complete reprinting of *Drawings of Frederic Remington* (1897), plus other selections. 4 additional drawings in color on covers. 140pp. 9 x 12. 20714-5 Pa. $3.95

EARLY NEW ENGLAND GRAVESTONE RUBBINGS, Edmund V. Gillon, Jr. 43 photographs, 226 rubbings show heavily symbolic, macabre, sometimes humorous primitive American art. Up to early 19th century. 207pp. 8⅜ x 11¼.
21380-3 Pa. $4.00

L.J.M. DAGUERRE: THE HISTORY OF THE DIORAMA AND THE DAGUERREOTYPE, Helmut and Alison Gernsheim. Definitive account. Early history, life and work of Daguerre; discovery of daguerreotype process; diffusion abroad; other early photography. 124 illustrations. 226pp. 6⅙ x 9¼.
22290-X Pa. $4.00

PHOTOGRAPHY AND THE AMERICAN SCENE, Robert Taft. The basic book on American photography as art, recording form, 1839-1889. Development, influence on society, great photographers, types (portraits, war, frontier, etc.), whatever else needed. Inexhaustible. Illustrated with 322 early photos, daguerreotypes, tintypes, stereo slides, etc. 546pp. 6⅛ x 9¼.
21201-7 Pa. $5.00

PHOTOGRAPHIC SKETCHBOOK OF THE CIVIL WAR, Alexander Gardner. Reproduction of 1866 volume with 100 on-the-field photographs: Manassas, Lincoln on battlefield, slave pens, etc. Introduction by E.F. Bleiler. 224pp. 10¾ x 9.
22731-6 Pa. $4.50

THE MOVIES: A PICTURE QUIZ BOOK, Stanley Appelbaum & Hayward Cirker. Match stars with their movies, name actors and actresses, test your movie skill with 241 stills from 236 great movies, 1902-1959. Indexes of performers and films. 128pp. 8⅜ x 9¼.
20222-4 Pa. $2.50

THE TALKIES, Richard Griffith. Anthology of features, articles from Photoplay, 1928-1940, reproduced complete. Stars, famous movies, technical features, fabulous ads, etc.; Garbo, Chaplin, King Kong, Lubitsch, etc. 4 color plates, scores of illustrations. 327pp. 8⅜ x 11¼.
22762-6 Pa. $5.95

THE MOVIE MUSICAL FROM VITAPHONE TO "42ND STREET," edited by Miles Kreuger. Relive the rise of the movie musical as reported in the pages of Photoplay magazine (1926-1933): every movie review, cast list, ad, and record review; every significant feature article, production still, biography, forecast, and gossip story. Profusely illustrated. 367pp. 8⅜ x 11¼.
23154-2 Pa. $6.95

JOHANN SEBASTIAN BACH, Philipp Spitta. Great classic of biography, musical commentary, with hundreds of pieces analyzed. Also good for Bach's contemporaries. 450 musical examples. Total of 1799pp.
EUK 22278-0, 22279-9 Clothbd., Two vol. set $25.00

BEETHOVEN AND HIS NINE SYMPHONIES, Sir George Grove. Thorough history, analysis, commentary on symphonies and some related pieces. For either beginner or advanced student. 436 musical passages. 407pp.
20334-4 Pa. $4.00

MOZART AND HIS PIANO CONCERTOS, Cuthbert Girdlestone. The only full-length study. Detailed analyses of all 21 concertos, sources; 417 musical examples. 509pp.
21271-8 Pa. $4.50

THE FITZWILLIAM VIRGINAL BOOK, edited by J. Fuller Maitland, W.B. Squire. Famous early 17th century collection of keyboard music, 300 works by Morley, Byrd, Bull, Gibbons, etc. Modern notation. Total of 938pp. 8⅜ x 11.
ECE 21068-5, 21069-3 Pa., Two vol. set $12.00

COMPLETE STRING QUARTETS, Wolfgang A. Mozart. Breitkopf and Härtel edition. All 23 string quartets plus alternate slow movement to K156. Study score. 277pp. 9⅜ x 12¼.
22372-8 Pa. $6.00

COMPLETE SONG CYCLES, Franz Schubert. Complete piano, vocal music of Die Schöne Müllerin, Die Winterreise, Schwanengesang. Also Drinker English singing translations. Breitkopf and Härtel edition. 217pp. 9⅜ x 12¼.
22649-2 Pa. $4.00

THE COMPLETE PRELUDES AND ETUDES FOR PIANOFORTE SOLO, Alexander Scriabin. All the preludes and etudes including many perfectly spun miniatures. Edited by K.N. Igumnov and Y.I. Mil'shteyn. 250pp. 9 x 12.
22919-X Pa. $5.00

TRISTAN UND ISOLDE, Richard Wagner. Full orchestral score with complete instrumentation. Do not confuse with piano reduction. Commentary by Felix Mottl, great Wagnerian conductor and scholar. Study score. 655pp. 8⅛ x 11.
22915-7 Pa. $10.00

FAVORITE SONGS OF THE NINETIES, ed. Robert Fremont. Full reproduction, including covers, of 88 favorites: Ta-Ra-Ra-Boom-De-Aye, The Band Played On, Bird in a Gilded Cage, Under the Bamboo Tree, After the Ball, etc. 401pp. 9 x 12.
EBE 21536-9 Pa. $6.95

SOUSA'S GREAT MARCHES IN PIANO TRANSCRIPTION: ORIGINAL SHEET MUSIC OF 23 WORKS, John Philip Sousa. Selected by Lester S. Levy. Playing edition includes: The Stars and Stripes Forever, The Thunderer, The Gladiator, King Cotton, Washington Post, much more. 24 illustrations. 111pp. 9 x 12.
USO 23132-1 Pa. $3.50

CLASSIC PIANO RAGS, selected with an introduction by Rudi Blesh. Best ragtime music (1897-1922) by Scott Joplin, James Scott, Joseph F. Lamb, Tom Turpin, 9 others. Printed from best original sheet music, plus covers. 364pp. 9 x 12.
EBE 20469-3 Pa. $6.95

ANALYSIS OF CHINESE CHARACTERS, C.D. Wilder, J.H. Ingram. 1000 most important characters analyzed according to primitives, phonetics, historical development. Traditional method offers mnemonic aid to beginner, intermediate student of Chinese, Japanese. 365pp.
23045-7 Pa. $4.00

MODERN CHINESE: A BASIC COURSE, Faculty of Peking University. Self study, · classroom course in modern Mandarin. Records contain phonetics, vocabulary, sentences, lessons. 249 page book contains all recorded text, translations, grammar, vocabulary, exercises. Best course on market. 3 12" 33⅓ monaural records, book, album.
98832-5 Set $12.50

THE BEST DR. THORNDYKE DETECTIVE STORIES, R. Austin Freeman. The Case of Oscar Brodski, The Moabite Cipher, and 5 other favorites featuring the great scientific detective, plus his long-believed-lost first adventure — 31 New Inn — reprinted here for the first time. Edited by E.F. Bleiler. USO 20388-3 Pa. $3.00

BEST "THINKING MACHINE" DETECTIVE STORIES, Jacques Futrelle. The Problem of Cell 13 and 11 other stories about Prof. Augustus S.F.X. Van Dusen, including two "lost" stories. First reprinting of several. Edited by E.F. Bleiler. 241pp. 20537-1 Pa. $3.00

UNCLE SILAS, J. Sheridan LeFanu. Victorian Gothic mystery novel, considered by many best of period, even better than Collins or Dickens. Wonderful psychological terror. Introduction by Frederick Shroyer. 436pp. 21715-9 Pa. $4.00

BEST DR. POGGIOLI DETECTIVE STORIES, T.S. Stribling. 15 best stories from EQMM and The Saint offer new adventures in Mexico, Florida, Tennessee hills as Poggioli unravels mysteries and combats Count Jalacki. 217pp. 23227-1 Pa. $3.00

EIGHT DIME NOVELS, selected with an introduction by E.F. Bleiler. Adventures of Old King Brady, Frank James, Nick Carter, Deadwood Dick, Buffalo Bill, The Steam Man, Frank Merriwell, and Horatio Alger — 1877 to 1905. Important, entertaining popular literature in facsimile reprint, with original covers. 190pp. 9 x 12. 22975-0 Pa. $3.50

ALICE'S ADVENTURES UNDER GROUND, Lewis Carroll. Facsimile of ms. Carroll gave Alice Liddell in 1864. Different in many ways from final Alice. Handlettered, illustrated by Carroll. Introduction by Martin Gardner. 128pp. 21482-6 Pa. $1.50

ALICE IN WONDERLAND COLORING BOOK, Lewis Carroll. Pictures by John Tenniel. Large-size versions of the famous illustrations of Alice, Cheshire Cat, Mad Hatter and all the others, waiting for your crayons. Abridged text. 36 illustrations. 64pp. 8¼ x 11. 22853-3 Pa. $1.50

AVENTURES D'ALICE AU PAYS DES MERVEILLES, Lewis Carroll. Bué's translation of "Alice" into French, supervised by Carroll himself. Novel way to learn language. (No English text.) 42 Tenniel illustrations. 196pp. 22836-3 Pa. $2.00

MYTHS AND FOLK TALES OF IRELAND, Jeremiah Curtin. 11 stories that are Irish versions of European fairy tales and 9 stories from the Fenian cycle — 20 tales of legend and magic that comprise an essential work in the history of folklore. 256pp. 22430-9 Pa. $3.00

EAST O' THE SUN AND WEST O' THE MOON, George W. Dasent. Only full edition of favorite, wonderful Norwegian fairytales — Why the Sea is Salt, Boots and the Troll, etc. — with 77 illustrations by Kittelsen & Werenskiöld. 418pp. 22521-6 Pa. $3.50

PERRAULT'S FAIRY TALES, Charles Perrault and Gustave Doré. Original versions of Cinderella, Sleeping Beauty, Little Red Riding Hood, etc. in best translation, with 34 wonderful illustrations by Gustave Doré. 117pp. 8⅛ x 11. 22311-6 Pa. $2.50

MOTHER GOOSE'S MELODIES. Facsimile of fabulously rare Munroe and Francis "copyright 1833" Boston edition. Familiar and unusual rhymes, wonderful old woodcut illustrations. Edited by E.F. Bleiler. 128pp. 4½ x 6⅜. 22577-1 Pa. $1.00

MOTHER GOOSE IN HIEROGLYPHICS. Favorite nursery rhymes presented in rebus form for children. Fascinating 1849 edition reproduced in toto, with key. Introduction by E.F. Bleiler. About 400 woodcuts. 64pp. 6⅞ x 5¼. 20745-5 Pa. $1.00

PETER PIPER'S PRACTICAL PRINCIPLES OF PLAIN & PERFECT PRONUNCIATION. Alliterative jingles and tongue-twisters. Reproduction in full of 1830 first American edition. 25 spirited woodcuts. 32pp. 4½ x 6⅜. 22560-7 Pa. $1.00

MARMADUKE MULTIPLY'S MERRY METHOD OF MAKING MINOR MATHEMATICIANS. Fellow to Peter Piper, it teaches multiplication table by catchy rhymes and woodcuts. 1841 Munroe & Francis edition. Edited by E.F. Bleiler. 103pp. 4⅝ x 6.
22773-1 Pa. $1.25
20171-6 Clothbd. $3.00

THE NIGHT BEFORE CHRISTMAS, Clement Moore. Full text, and woodcuts from original 1848 book. Also critical, historical material. 19 illustrations. 40pp. 4⅝ x 6. 22797-9 Pa. $1.00

THE KING OF THE GOLDEN RIVER, John Ruskin. Victorian children's classic of three brothers, their attempts to reach the Golden River, what becomes of them. Facsimile of original 1889 edition. 22 illustrations. 56pp. 4⅝ x 6⅜.
20066-3 Pa. $1.25

DREAMS OF THE RAREBIT FIEND, Winsor McCay. Pioneer cartoon strip, unexcelled for beauty, imagination, in 60 full sequences. Incredible technical virtuosity, wonderful visual wit. Historical introduction. 62pp. 8⅜ x 11¼. 21347-1 Pa. $2.00

THE KATZENJAMMER KIDS, Rudolf Dirks. In full color, 14 strips from 1906-7; full of imagination, characteristic humor. Classic of great historical importance. Introduction by August Derleth. 32pp. 9¼ x 12¼. 23005-8 Pa. $2.00

LITTLE ORPHAN ANNIE AND LITTLE ORPHAN ANNIE IN COSMIC CITY, Harold Gray. Two great sequences from the early strips: our curly-haired heroine defends the Warbucks' financial empire and, then, takes on meanie Phineas P. Pinchpenny. Leapin' lizards! 178pp. 6⅛ x 8⅜. 23107-0 Pa. $2.00

WHEN A FELLER NEEDS A FRIEND, Clare Briggs. 122 cartoons by one of the greatest newspaper cartoonists of the early 20th century — about growing up, making a living, family life, daily frustrations and occasional triumphs. 121pp. 8½ x 9½.
23148-8 Pa. $2.50

THE BEST OF GLUYAS WILLIAMS. 100 drawings by one of America's finest cartoonists: The Day a Cake of Ivory Soap Sank at Proctor & Gamble's, At the Life Insurance Agents' Banquet, and many other gems from the 20's and 30's. 118pp. 8⅜ x 11¼. 22737-5 Pa. $2.50

THE MAGIC MOVING PICTURE BOOK, Bliss, Sands & Co. The pictures in this book move! Volcanoes erupt, a house burns, a serpentine dancer wiggles her way through a number. By using a specially ruled acetate screen provided, you can obtain these and 15 other startling effects. Originally "The Motograph Moving Picture Book." 32pp. 8¼ x 11.   23224-7 Pa. $1.75

STRING FIGURES AND HOW TO MAKE THEM, Caroline F. Jayne. Fullest, clearest instructions on string figures from around world: Eskimo, Navajo, Lapp, Europe, more. Cats cradle, moving spear, lightning, stars. Introduction by A.C. Haddon. 950 illustrations. 407pp.   20152-X Pa. $3.00

PAPER FOLDING FOR BEGINNERS, William D. Murray and Francis J. Rigney. Clearest book on market for making origami sail boats, roosters, frogs that move legs, cups, bonbon boxes. 40 projects. More than 275 illustrations. Photographs. 94pp.
20713-7 Pa. $1.25

INDIAN SIGN LANGUAGE, William Tomkins. Over 525 signs developed by Sioux, Blackfoot, Cheyenne, Arapahoe and other tribes. Written instructions and diagrams: how to make words, construct sentences. Also 290 pictographs of Sioux and Ojibway tribes. 111pp. 6⅛ x 9¼.   22029-X Pa. $1.50

BOOMERANGS: HOW TO MAKE AND THROW THEM, Bernard S. Mason. Easy to make and throw, dozens of designs: cross-stick, pinwheel, boomabird, tumblestick, Australian curved stick boomerang. Complete throwing instructions. All safe. 99pp.   23028-7 Pa. $1.50

25 KITES THAT FLY, Leslie Hunt. Full, easy to follow instructions for kites made from inexpensive materials. Many novelties. Reeling, raising, designing your own. 70 illustrations. 110pp.   22550-X Pa. $1.25

TRICKS AND GAMES ON THE POOL TABLE, Fred Herrmann. 79 tricks and games, some solitaires, some for 2 or more players, some competitive; mystifying shots and throws, unusual carom, tricks involving cork, coins, a hat, more. 77 figures. 95pp.   21814-7 Pa. $1.25

WOODCRAFT AND CAMPING, Bernard S. Mason. How to make a quick emergency shelter, select woods that will burn immediately, make do with limited supplies, etc. Also making many things out of wood, rawhide, bark, at camp. Formerly titled Woodcraft. 295 illustrations. 580pp.   21951-8 Pa. $4.00

AN INTRODUCTION TO CHESS MOVES AND TACTICS SIMPLY EXPLAINED, Leonard Barden. Informal intermediate introduction: reasons for moves, tactics, openings, traps, positional play, endgame. Isolates patterns. 102pp. USO 21210-6 Pa. $1.35

LASKER'S MANUAL OF CHESS, Dr. Emanuel Lasker. Great world champion offers very thorough coverage of all aspects of chess. Combinations, position play, openings, endgame, aesthetics of chess, philosophy of struggle, much more. Filled with analyzed games. 390pp.   20640-8 Pa. $3.50

CATALOGUE OF DOVER BOOKS

How to Solve Chess Problems, Kenneth S. Howard. Practical suggestions on problem solving for very beginners. 58 two-move problems, 46 3-movers, 8 4-movers for practice, plus hints. 171pp. 20748-X Pa. $2.00

A Guide to Fairy Chess, Anthony Dickins. 3-D chess, 4-D chess, chess on a cylindrical board, reflecting pieces that bounce off edges, cooperative chess, retrograde chess, maximummers, much more. Most based on work of great Dawson. Full handbook, 100 problems. 66pp. 7⅞ x 10¾. 22687-5 Pa. $2.00

Win at Backgammon, Millard Hopper. Best opening moves, running game, blocking game, back game, tables of odds, etc. Hopper makes the game clear enough for anyone to play, and win. 43 diagrams. 111pp. 22894-0 Pa. $1.50

Bidding a Bridge Hand, Terence Reese. Master player "thinks out loud" the binding of 75 hands that defy point count systems. Organized by bidding problem—no-fit situations, overbidding, underbidding, cueing your defense, etc. 254pp. EBE 22830-4 Pa. $2.50

The Precision Bidding System in Bridge, C.C. Wei, edited by Alan Truscott. Inventor of precision bidding presents average hands and hands from actual play, including games from 1969 Bermuda Bowl where system emerged. 114 exercises. 116pp. 21171-1 Pa. $1.75

Learn Magic, Henry Hay. 20 simple, easy-to-follow lessons on magic for the new magician: illusions, card tricks, silks, sleights of hand, coin manipulations, escapes, and more —all with a minimum amount of equipment. Final chapter explains the great stage illusions. 92 illustrations. 285pp. 21238-6 Pa. $2.95

The New Magician's Manual, Walter B. Gibson. Step-by-step instructions and clear illustrations guide the novice in mastering 36 tricks; much equipment supplied on 16 pages of cut-out materials. 36 additional tricks. 64 illustrations. 159pp. 6⅝ x 10. 23113-5 Pa. $3.00

Professional Magic for Amateurs, Walter B. Gibson. 50 easy, effective tricks used by professionals —cards, string, tumblers, handkerchiefs, mental magic, etc. 63 illustrations. 223pp. 23012-0 Pa. $2.50

Card Manipulations, Jean Hugard. Very rich collection of manipulations; has taught thousands of fine magicians tricks that are really workable, eye-catching. Easily followed, serious work. Over 200 illustrations. 163pp. 20539-8 Pa. $2.00

Abbott's Encyclopedia of Rope Tricks for Magicians, Stewart James. Complete reference book for amateur and professional magicians containing more than 150 tricks involving knots, penetrations, cut and restored rope, etc. 510 illustrations. Reprint of 3rd edition. 400pp. 23206-9 Pa. $3.50

The Secrets of Houdini, J.C. Cannell. Classic study of Houdini's incredible magic, exposing closely-kept professional secrets and revealing, in general terms, the whole art of stage magic. 67 illustrations. 279pp. 22913-0 Pa. $2.50

DRIED FLOWERS, Sarah Whitlock and Martha Rankin. Concise, clear, practical guide to dehydration, glycerinizing, pressing plant material, and more. Covers use of silica gel. 12 drawings. Originally titled "New Techniques with Dried Flowers." 32pp. 21802-3 Pa. $1.00

ABC OF POULTRY RAISING, J.H. Florea. Poultry expert, editor tells how to raise chickens on home or small business basis. Breeds, feeding, housing, laying, etc. Very concrete, practical. 50 illustrations. 256pp. 23201-8 Pa. $3.00

HOW INDIANS USE WILD PLANTS FOR FOOD, MEDICINE & CRAFTS, Frances Densmore. Smithsonian, Bureau of American Ethnology report presents wealth of material on nearly 200 plants used by Chippewas of Minnesota and Wisconsin. 33 plates plus 122pp. of text. 6⅛ x 9¼. 23019-8 Pa. $2.50

THE HERBAL OR GENERAL HISTORY OF PLANTS, John Gerard. The 1633 edition revised and enlarged by Thomas Johnson. Containing almost 2850 plant descriptions and 2705 superb illustrations, Gerard's Herbal is a monumental work, the book all modern English herbals are derived from, and the one herbal every serious enthusiast should have in its entirety. Original editions are worth perhaps $750. 1678pp. 8½ x 12¼. 23147-X Clothbd. $50.00

A MODERN HERBAL, Margaret Grieve. Much the fullest, most exact, most useful compilation of herbal material. Gigantic alphabetical encyclopedia, from aconite to zedoary, gives botanical information, medical properties, folklore, economic uses, and much else. Indispensable to serious reader. 161 illustrations. 888pp. 6½ x 9¼. USO 22798-7, 22799-5 Pa., Two vol. set $10.00

HOW TO KNOW THE FERNS, Frances T. Parsons. Delightful classic. Identification, fern lore, for Eastern and Central U.S.A. Has introduced thousands to interesting life form. 99 illustrations. 215pp. 20740-4 Pa. $2.50

THE MUSHROOM HANDBOOK, Louis C.C. Krieger. Still the best popular handbook. Full descriptions of 259 species, extremely thorough text, habitats, luminescence, poisons, folklore, etc. 32 color plates; 126 other illustrations. 560pp. 21861-9 Pa. $4.50

HOW TO KNOW THE WILD FRUITS, Maude G. Peterson. Classic guide covers nearly 200 trees, shrubs, smaller plants of the U.S. arranged by color of fruit and then by family. Full text provides names, descriptions, edibility, uses. 80 illustrations. 400pp. 22943-2 Pa. $3.00

COMMON WEEDS OF THE UNITED STATES, U.S. Department of Agriculture. Covers 220 important weeds with illustration, maps, botanical information, plant lore for each. Over 225 illustrations. 463pp. 6⅛ x 9¼. 20504-5 Pa. $4.50

HOW TO KNOW THE WILD FLOWERS, Mrs. William S. Dana. Still best popular book for East and Central USA. Over 500 plants easily identified, with plant lore; arranged according to color and flowering time. 174 plates. 459pp. 20332-8 Pa. $3.50

MANUAL OF THE TREES OF NORTH AMERICA, Charles S. Sargent. The basic survey of every native tree and tree-like shrub, 717 species in all. Extremely full descriptions, information on habitat, growth, locales, economics, etc. Necessary to every serious tree lover. Over 100 finding keys. 783 illustrations. Total of 986pp.
20277-1, 20278-X Pa., Two vol. set $8.00

BIRDS OF THE NEW YORK AREA, John Bull. Indispensable guide to more than 400 species within a hundred-mile radius of Manhattan. Information on range, status, breeding, migration, distribution trends, etc. Foreword by Roger Tory Peterson. 17 drawings; maps. 540pp. 23222-0 Pa. $6.00

THE SEA-BEACH AT EBB-TIDE, Augusta Foote Arnold. Identify hundreds of marine plants and animals: algae, seaweeds, squids, crabs, corals, etc. Descriptions cover food, life cycle, size, shape, habitat. Over 600 drawings. 490pp.
21949-6 Pa. $4.00

THE MOTH BOOK, William J. Holland. Identify more than 2,000 moths of North America. General information, precise species descriptions. 623 illustrations plus 48 color plates show almost all species, full size. 1968 edition. Still the basic book. Total of 551pp. 6½ x 9¼. 21948-8 Pa. $6.00

AN INTRODUCTION TO THE REPTILES AND AMPHIBIANS OF THE UNITED STATES, Percy A. Morris. All lizards, crocodiles, turtles, snakes, toads, frogs; life history, identification, habits, suitability as pets, etc. Non-technical, but sound and broad. 130 photos. 253pp. 22982-3 Pa. $3.00

OLD NEW YORK IN EARLY PHOTOGRAPHS, edited by Mary Black. Your only chance to see New York City as it was 1853-1906, through 196 wonderful photographs from N.Y. Historical Society. Great Blizzard, Lincoln's funeral procession, great buildings. 228pp. 9 x 12. 22907-6 Pa. $6.00

THE AMERICAN REVOLUTION, A PICTURE SOURCEBOOK, John Grafton. Wonderful Bicentennial picture source, with 411 illustrations (contemporary and 19th century) showing battles, personalities, maps, events, flags, posters, soldier's life, ships, etc. all captioned and explained. A wonderful browsing book, supplement to other historical reading. 160pp. 9 x 12. 23226-3 Pa. $4.00

PERSONAL NARRATIVE OF A PILGRIMAGE TO AL-MADINAH AND MECCAH, Richard Burton. Great travel classic by remarkably colorful personality. Burton, disguised as a Moroccan, visited sacred shrines of Islam, narrowly escaping death. Wonderful observations of Islamic life, customs, personalities. 47 illustrations. Total of 959pp. 21217-3, 21218-1 Pa., Two vol. set $7.00

INCIDENTS OF TRAVEL IN CENTRAL AMERICA, CHIAPAS, AND YUCATAN, John L. Stephens. Almost single-handed discovery of Maya culture; exploration of ruined cities, monuments, temples; customs of Indians. 115 drawings. 892pp.
22404-X, 22405-8 Pa., Two vol. set $8.00

HOUDINI ON MAGIC, Harold Houdini. Edited by Walter Gibson, Morris N. Young. How he escaped; exposés of fake spiritualists; instructions for eye-catching tricks; other fascinating material by and about greatest magician. 155 illustrations. 280pp. 20384-0 Pa. $2.50

HANDBOOK OF THE NUTRITIONAL CONTENTS OF FOOD, U.S. Dept. of Agriculture. Largest, most detailed source of food nutrition information ever prepared. Two mammoth tables: one measuring nutrients in 100 grams of edible portion; the other, in edible portion of 1 pound as purchased. Originally titled Composition of Foods. 190pp. 9 x 12. 21342-0 Pa. $4.00

COMPLETE GUIDE TO HOME CANNING, PRESERVING AND FREEZING, U.S. Dept. of Agriculture. Seven basic manuals with full instructions for jams and jellies; pickles and relishes; canning fruits, vegetables, meat; freezing anything. Really good recipes, exact instructions for optimal results. Save a fortune in food. 156 illustrations. 214pp. 6^1/$_8$ x 9^1/$_4$. 22911-4 Pa. $2.50

THE BREAD TRAY, Louis P. De Gouy. Nearly every bread the cook could buy or make: bread sticks of Italy, fruit breads of Greece, glazed rolls of Vienna, everything from corn pone to croissants. Over 500 recipes altogether. including buns, rolls, muffins, scones, and more. 463pp. 23000-7 Pa. $3.50

CREATIVE HAMBURGER COOKERY, Louis P. De Gouy. 182 unusual recipes for casseroles, meat loaves and hamburgers that turn inexpensive ground meat into memorable main dishes: Arizona chili burgers, burger tamale pie, burger stew, burger corn loaf, burger wine loaf, and more. 120pp. 23001-5 Pa. $1.75

LONG ISLAND SEAFOOD COOKBOOK, J. George Frederick and Jean Joyce. Probably the best American seafood cookbook. Hundreds of recipes. 40 gourmet sauces, 123 recipes using oysters alone! All varieties of fish and seafood amply represented. 324pp. 22677-8 Pa. $3.00

THE EPICUREAN: A COMPLETE TREATISE OF ANALYTICAL AND PRACTICAL STUDIES IN THE CULINARY ART, Charles Ranhofer. Great modern classic. 3,500 recipes from master chef of Delmonico's, turn-of-the-century America's best restaurant. Also explained, many techniques known only to professional chefs. 775 illustrations. 1183pp. 6^5/$_8$ x 10. 22680-8 Clothbd. $17.50

THE AMERICAN WINE COOK BOOK, Ted Hatch. Over 700 recipes: old favorites livened up with wine plus many more: Czech fish soup, quince soup, sauce Perigueux, shrimp shortcake, filets Stroganoff, cordon bleu goulash, jambonneau, wine fruit cake, more. 314pp. 22796-0 Pa. $2.50

DELICIOUS VEGETARIAN COOKING, Ivan Baker. Close to 500 delicious and varied recipes: soups, main course dishes (pea, bean, lentil, cheese, vegetable, pasta, and egg dishes), savories, stews, whole-wheat breads and cakes, more. 168pp. USO 22834-7 Pa. $1.75

COOKIES FROM MANY LANDS, Josephine Perry. Crullers, oatmeal cookies, chaux au chocolate, English tea cakes, mandel kuchen, Sacher torte, Danish puff pastry, Swedish cookies — a mouth-watering collection of 223 recipes. 157pp.
22832-0 Pa. $2.00

ROSE RECIPES, Eleanour S. Rohde. How to make sauces, jellies, tarts, salads, potpourris, sweet bags, pomanders, perfumes from garden roses; all exact recipes. Century old favorites. 95pp.
22957-2 Pa. $1.25

"OSCAR" OF THE WALDORF'S COOKBOOK, Oscar Tschirky. Famous American chef reveals 3455 recipes that made Waldorf great; cream of French, German, American cooking, in all categories. Full instructions, easy home use. 1896 edition. 907pp. 6⅝ x 9⅜.
20790-0 Clothbd. $15.00

JAMS AND JELLIES, May Byron. Over 500 old-time recipes for delicious jams, jellies, marmalades, preserves, and many other items. Probably the largest jam and jelly book in print. Originally titled May Byron's Jam Book. 276pp.
USO 23130-5 Pa. $3.00

MUSHROOM RECIPES, André L. Simon. 110 recipes for everyday and special cooking. Champignons à la grecque, sole bonne femme, chicken liver croustades, more; 9 basic sauces, 13 ways of cooking mushrooms. 54pp.
USO 20913-X Pa. $1.25

FAVORITE SWEDISH RECIPES, edited by Sam Widenfelt. Prepared in Sweden, offers wonderful, clearly explained Swedish dishes: appetizers, meats, pastry and cookies, other categories. Suitable for American kitchen. 90 photos. 157pp.
23156-9 Pa. $2.00

THE BUCKEYE COOKBOOK, Buckeye Publishing Company. Over 1,000 easy-to-follow, traditional recipes from the American Midwest: bread (100 recipes alone), meat, game, jam, candy, cake, ice cream, and many other categories of cooking. 64 illustrations. From 1883 enlarged edition. 416pp.
23218-2 Pa. $4.00

TWENTY-TWO AUTHENTIC BANQUETS FROM INDIA, Robert H. Christie. Complete, easy-to-do recipes for almost 200 authentic Indian dishes assembled in 22 banquets. Arranged by region. Selected from Banquets of the Nations. 192pp.
23200-X Pa. $2.50